"In this book, Mr. McKi[n] [...] instructional methods that guide your students to learn from, become, and share like experts in ways so engaging they'll be okay with missing recess!"

-ELISABETH STAYER, SCHOOL LIBRARIAN &
EDUCATOR

"We live in interesting times. This book provides tangible ways that you as a teacher can develop your teaching to improve the outcomes for your learners. The importance of connection is highlighted in order that our profession continues to develop and improve."

-DR. MICHAEL HARVEY, SCIENCE EDUCATOR

"In this book, Grayson and Zach lay the groundwork regarding "schooling vs. learning" and generously share their experiences as classroom teachers using project-based learning as part of their delivery system. The book is steeped with concrete examples and tools that will validate, extend, and challenge us as educators to continue to strive to reach all students."

-LARRY THOMAS, EDUCATIONAL CONSULTANT

"*The Expert Effect* paints a compelling picture of what joyful learning can look like in the classroom. Grayson and Zach offer teachers practical tips for designing learning experiences that foster a learning culture by prioritizing authenticity and student voice and choice. If you are looking for ways to empower your students to thrive in a complex world, this book has the answer!"

-JENNIFER GOTTLIEB, EXECUTIVE DIRECTOR FOR
DISTRICT & SCHOOL SERVICES

"I appreciate a lot of the suggestions recommended to teachers in this book. From my experience, it really makes class fun and interesting. Mr. Rondot and Mr. McKinney use their own experience to show how easy these techniques are. I love how they encourage teachers to lift up their students' voices so that they are heard in the classroom."

—GARVEY MORTLEY, STUDENT ACTIVIST,
PODCASTER & GAMER

"I met Grayson McKinney's Grade 4 students several years ago when they were the "experts" during a presentation I was giving. They exhibited confidence and poise speaking to an audience of adults! *The Expert Effect* blends research, classroom experiences, and best practices to inspire and guide you in your own journey to amplify the voices of your own students by connecting them to experts."

—JENNIFER CASA-TODD, TEACHER-LIBRARIAN &
AUTHOR

"This book is full of big ideas with detailed ways to achieve them. Zach and Grayson share how to design authentic learning, connect with professionals, take learning outside of the classroom, empower students, and develop the mindset in students that they are capable of dynamic and expert-level work."

—TREVOR MUIR, EDUCATOR & AUTHOR

THE EXPERT EFFECT

A THREE-PART SYSTEM TO BREAK DOWN THE
WALLS OF YOUR CLASSROOM AND CONNECT
YOUR STUDENTS TO THE WORLD

GRAYSON MCKINNEY, ED.S.

ZACH RONDOT, M.A.

EduMatch Publishing

CONTENTS

This work is dedicated to the youthful memory and inquisitive spirit of the hundreds of children that have walked into our classrooms and lives over the last two decades. To the "innovators" and the "futurists" among us, thank you for sharing your laughter and learning with us. Thank you for always being willing to indulge our crazy ideas and just "go along with it." It is with the hope that by giving other teachers around the world a glimpse into our classrooms, we can inspire change in the system and make the world of education a better place. Without you, none of this would be worthwhile or possible. We are honored to dedicate this book to all the students we have served who have always been brave enough to speak up and be heard.

–Mr. Rondot & Mr. McKinney

ACKNOWLEDGMENTS

I (Grayson) need to thank and acknowledge my wonderful wife, Briona, for all of the support and encouragement. Without you cheering me on and constantly pushing me to do something amazing, I would be living a much more boring life. Thank you for being my firecracker and for lighting a fire under me. Your passion and wisdom have always helped cut to the heart of any matter, and I am in constant awe of your dedication and service to others. You make me work harder, make me smarter, and make me remember why I'm here. I am eternally grateful that Lochlan, Dempsey, and Madigan have you as their mother because you will always be someone who will drive our family in the right direction. I love you! Thank you to my brother for your encouragement and input. Your equanimity and eternal optimism have always been inspirational to me. Your help on this project, in particular, was invaluable, and I truly appreciate your wisdom and guidance. Thank you, also, to my incredibly strong and inspirational mom. Thank you for always being my biggest fan and for always making me feel like I could do anything. Your sacrifices for our family and the unconditional love you continue to give are worth more than words can say. Thank you.

I (Zach) need to acknowledge my amazing family, who have always encouraged me and inspired me. I am lucky to come from a family with deep roots in education. My grandparents met while teaching down the hall from each other in Detroit Public Schools in the mid 1950s. It may sound cliché to say, but my mom and grandmother were literally my first teachers. In 1983, they opened Mon Ami Daycare and Nursery School and have given the gift of early education to countless young learners over the years. Without these roots in education, I do not think I would be writing this today. I also need to thank my dad for teaching me the power of positivity and encouraging me in all aspects of life.

We both need to acknowledge and thank our principal, Dr. Tammy DiPonio. Tammy not only hired both of us into the Troy School District, where student thinking is visible, valued, and actively promoted, but also gave us so many opportunities to take risks in our teaching practice. Time after time, her answer was, "yes, and…" which helped us grow as teachers and showed us through her support that education can and always should be more.

We didn't get to be where we are today on our own, and we owe much to our special learning community. An enormous thank you needs to be given to our teaching partners and colleagues at Costello Elementary, who have always been more than willing to indulge our grand ambitions and support our students in their endeavors to share new-found knowledge. Go Cardinals!

We also wish to thank our global partners who served as an intellectual sounding board during the development of *The Expert Effect*. Specifically, we want to thank Trevor Muir at Grand Valley State University, Elisabeth Stayer at The Roeper School, Jennifer Casa-Todd at Cardinal Carter Catholic High School, and Dr. Michael Harvey at Marlborough College Malaysia. Thank you for your care and commitment to this project.

Finally, we also need to say a special thank you to Dr. Sarah Thomas and the other global educators at EduMatch Publishing. Thank you for believing in us and for your mentorship that has set us on this path towards revolutionizing the way children learn and the way teachers teach. We are grateful and proud to count ourselves among your collaborative cohort.

FOREWORD

I became a teacher because I didn't like school.

It's not that I didn't believe in school; it's that I did believe in it, or at least its potential. My personal school experience was largely occupied with rote memorization, very little autonomy, textbooks, and grades—a one-size-fits-all system that didn't fit me. I rarely exercised my own creativity while sitting in rows listening to hour-long lectures that failed to inspire me. Getting good grades or making it into honors classes was hardly enough to get me to engage with school. And so I didn't, and mostly seemed to sleepwalk my way through twelve years of education.

But there were the rare learning experiences—the science fair project, the history reenactment, the trebuchet-building in physics class, the submissions to the town newspaper in English—that pulled me from my apathy as a student and showed me what inspired learning looks like. During these experiences, teachers became guides, leading me through hands-on encounters that required me to learn certain knowledge and skills in order to succeed. These rare units and projects gave me confidence. They got me excited about math or science class. They encouraged me to work hard in school and out of it when there was a looming deadline. They emboldened a young boy full of energy and potential and made him feel like an expert.

But times like these were also few and far between, so I became a teacher to make sure this wasn't the case for my students.

I quickly learned that big ideas, like creating authentic learning or promoting student empowerment, are great, but they require detail and processes to make them work. It's not enough to just want this for your students; you have to be able to design and create the type of learning that motivates, engages, and transforms lives.

In *The Expert Effect*, Grayson and Zach help educators discover how to do this. Using practical tips, ideas, and stories, they lay out a process that any teacher can use to engage students. When we treat learners as potential experts and give them opportunities to do real work that actually matters, they can excel in ways they never could in a traditional school format. From creating authentic projects, connecting with experts outside of school, to presenting student work to the community, *The Expert Effect* is really about how to make learning engaging for all students.

This book is full of big ideas with detailed ways to achieve them. Zach and Grayson share how to design authentic learning, connect with professionals, take learning outside of the classroom, empower students, and develop the mindset in students that they are capable of dynamic and expert-level work.

But this book is also about how teachers are experts too. We have a unique, high-level collection of skills and knowledge that can be used to create dynamic learning for our students. When teachers believe this and develop the "expert mindset," school becomes a place where all students can succeed. The learning that happens there is something students don't quickly forget—or like me as a child—dread. Instead, it's a place where students can thrive because they are treated as and led by experts.

–Trevor Muir

Trevor is a teacher, author, international speaker, and Project-Based Learning expert. He is the author of *The Epic Classroom: How to Boost Engagement, Make Learning Memorable, and Transform Lives*, a book about using the power of story to make learning engaging and unforgettable, as well as *The Collaborative Classroom: Teaching Students How to Work Together Now and for the Rest of Their Lives*.

Trevor is a professor at Grand Valley State University and a former faculty member for PBL Works. His writing has been featured in the Huffington Post, EdWeek, and regularly on WeAreTeachers. Trevor's Facebook page, The Epic Classroom, has inspiring videos that have been viewed over 25 million times. At the heart of Trevor's work is the conviction that every student has the potential for greatness, and every teacher can be equipped to unlock that potential. He is an overall outstanding educator and one who we are happy to call a mentor and friend. Follow him on Twitter: @TrevorMuir.

INTRODUCTION: OUR STORY

We know why you're here. You, like so many before you, are in search of something powerful and fundamental about what it means to be a better teacher, to make a greater impact on the students in your care, and to feel more fulfilled in your profession. We are like you, though at different waypoints, on the same path. We've never written a book before, but we thought it would provide a great opportunity for us to reflect on our own careers so far and help other people who would like to pursue a similar line of work. We're so glad you're here.

This journey started in September of 2013 on the third day of the school year when I, Zach, fresh out of college, entered what I hoped would be the last phase of my final teaching interview. The last hurdle was to teach a sample lesson to a real-life fourth-grade class. I walked into Grayson McKinney's classroom to teach my lesson about determining the meaning of unknown words in nonfiction texts. I guess you could say the lesson went well because just a few days later, we found ourselves as grade-level teaching partners. The rest, as they say, is history! If you would have told me walking into that interview that eight years later, we would be publishing a book together, there's no way I would have believed you. This book, essentially, is a culmination of everything that has happened since that fateful September day.

It didn't take long before we realized how like-minded we were as teaching partners—enthusiastic about technology integration in the classroom and willing to try just about any app to make learning "fun" and "engaging." This launched us into a partnership of collaborating to run sessions of professional development for teachers in our school district with workshop titles like, "So You Have iPads, Now What?" and "25 Apps You Need to Download Right Now for Literacy Integration," and "Top Ten Tech Tips for Teachers" (yes, we really did love alliteration). We admit it...we were caught up in the technology-craze of the day. We were all about giving our students the tools, but weren't yet setting them up with the authentic learning experiences to be successful.

Looking back, it is apparently clear that what we were providing then was more "technology training" than true professional learning. We had fallen into the trap of teaching with technology for technology's sake. We weren't yet reflecting on student learning outcomes as causation for technology integration. We just loved it all, as kids always do, because it was shiny and new. We have since discovered a more noble purpose for educational technology in the classroom, and we hope this book will illuminate that purpose for you as well as make amends for our "young and innocent" days.

In the 2016–17 school year, we embarked on our greatest educational challenge yet. As teachers, we have always been known to come up with some crazy ideas (just ask our students), but this would be the biggest risk we'd taken to date. In our school, there are removable dividing partitions between classrooms, so as the two fourth-grade teachers, we thought, "What if we removed that wall?" This idea was met by support from our administration, so we consulted the janitor, removed the wall, and the "4th-Grade Learning Lab" was born. One room. Two teachers. Fifty-six fourth graders.

This was truly a year that changed everything for us. Teaching is, by nature, an isolating profession—one adult by themselves in a room full of kids as the primary decision-maker (friends of ours in the business world are always amazed when we say teachers can't take bathroom breaks whenever they want). We flipped this paradigm on its head with our co-teaching concept (and it wasn't just for the bathroom break freedom).

How will students make their lunch choices in the morning? At which door do we line up to exit the classroom? How will we dismiss students back to their seats from the carpet? Simple decisions that normally were made in seconds by an individual teacher became lengthy, philosophical discussions. We realized that as similar as we were as teachers, we also had many differences. This was the moment we found out what "true collaboration" meant—we observed each other teach daily, provided feedback on lessons, and blended our educational philosophies to take the best ideas and approaches of both.

We started a blog that year and have since written extensively about the struggles we faced as well as the benefits of co-teaching at innovation4education.wordpress.com. But the biggest thing that came out of this experience was a newfound willingness to take risks in our teaching. With another professional to rely on for support and encouragement, we felt enabled to try things that may have been too risky or too grand in scale to take on solo. We were able to create an environment where kids were excited to get to school every day. School should be a place to which children want to come, not have to come, and taking big risks that *might* blow up in your face to create memorable activities gets them more excited than ever to come to school and learn valuable life lessons in the process.

SCHOOL SHOULD BE A PLACE TO WHICH CHILDREN WANT TO COME, NOT HAVE TO COME.
#ExpertEffectEDU

Then, another momentous shift happened. While planning our collaborative classroom, we spent a day learning from George Couros, an innovative Canadian educator and author of *The Innovator's Mindset: Empower Learning, Unleash Talent, and Lead a Culture of Creativity*, among other titles. One quote he shared with us that day rocked us to our core, "Technology will never replace great teachers, but technology in the hands of a great teacher can be transformational."

The reason we say that this was such a monumental event is that it opened our eyes to the fact that just because a kid can open an app on their iPad or has a classroom set of Chromebooks and can now type their responses into a word processor, it doesn't make what you're doing "innovative" or better than that which came before. In fact, we believe that using technology for technology's sake is not a worthy objective, but the new ways in which we will help you implement technology can and will be a game-changer. The big lesson we learned? Don't put the technological cart before the pedagogical horse. Use technology to enhance and deepen learning, not just to make your lesson look shiny to an observing administrator.

DON'T PUT THE TECHNOLOGICAL CART BEFORE THE PEDAGOGICAL HORSE.
#ExpertEffectEDU

So how do you avoid the pitfalls of being an overzealous "techhead" and hone in on just the stuff that will make the biggest impact on student learning and improve the educational experience? How do you embrace the philosophy of an educational risk-taker to create valuable learning opportunities that will stick with your learners long after they leave your room? We are so glad you asked! We're here to help you achieve the latter sentiment of Couros' famous phrase, "technology in the hands of a great teacher can be transformational."

Despite having closed the wall and gone our separate ways since Grayson moved up to teach fifth grade, our time spent co-teaching has stuck with us and continues to influence the way we plan our lessons, our units, and our years. The best parts of what came out of that "learning lab" will be outlined in this book, and we call our approach to this goal, *The Expert Effect*. Within these pages, we will expound upon a three-part pedagogy of how to get the students in your class to:

- **Learn from** experts outside the classroom
- **Become** experts through Project-Based Learning
- **Teach as** experts to an authentic audience

The choice to include technology or not is completely up to you. Leveraging digital platforms can act as a multiplier for the impact your teaching makes on your learners. It can extend your reach as you get your young scholars to share their learning with the world, and it can also shrink the distance between you and the experts that are out there to learn from. So, if you're comfortable with technology, go for it! Take the training wheels off. But if you're still dabbling and dipping in one toe at a time (sorry to mix metaphors), that's okay too. Think big, start small, but don't forget to think big in the first place! Hopefully, granting that permission helps you feel more comfortable easing into this new expert mindset while encouraging you to shoot for the stars...eventually.

So, rest assured that this book is not just for the tech-savvy. It's not just for the STEM enthusiast. It's not for the teacher at your building that everyone calls the overachiever or "wunderkind." Let us try saying it one other way: you don't necessarily need to be an *expert* in *anything* to be capable of tapping into the power of *The Expert Effect*. The real power comes from when you become an expert in taking a few risks and developing your willingness to try something new.

One of our friends and inspirations, Trevor Muir, gave a 2014 TEDx Talk titled "School Should Take Place in the Real World." In this talk, he says, "Instead of school being a giant hoop to jump through, a game, or even an obligation, it needs to be part of the real world." One thing you will never hear us say in our classrooms is anything that starts with "When you get to the real world...." When we teach with the mentality that what we're teaching will only benefit our students ten years down the road, we send the message that it's not important right now. I can't think of a faster way to turn kids off from learning than telling them something that won't be important for another fifteen years when they enter the "real world." Through this book, we aim to show you how to avoid this type of thinking and how to add authentic relevance to your content.

The true power of this book's ideas comes from breaking down the walls between what is *school* and what is *the world*. Whether it's learning from experts who come from outside your school or giving students the chance to teach like experts to an authentic audience outside the four walls of your classroom, building partnerships between your school and the greater community is a new necessity in education. *The Expert Effect* can help you see how to get started. Your community is full of professional people who are already experts in their own fields, ready to have their expertise drawn upon and used for the benefit of your learners. Even if you live in a tiny town with a population of thirty, then congratulations! Your community to solicit just became the entire world. That's what this book is about. No matter what you teach, where you are, or who you know, we want to connect your learners with the entire freakin' planet. Because if we can do it, you can too.

Lastly, we hope this book will be the start of a much greater conversation about the future and possibilities of education. Throughout the book, you will find a collection of "hyperlinks" that we especially appreciate and want to connect you to. These may include QR codes to scan with a smart device, URLs that you can manually type in to explore later, and the social media usernames of educators and organizations we respect and think you should follow. Unless we mention it specifically, all @-handles point you to experts' Twitter accounts, but some may indicate that they are on Instagram or Facebook instead.

You will also notice "Think & Tweet" questions at the end of each section. To make the most of your learning, we encourage you to share your expert experiences using the hashtag #ExpertEffectEDU. Don't forget to tag us—@GMcKinney2 and @MrRondot—in your tweets. We look forward to connecting with you! Thank you for joining us on this journey. Buckle up your seatbelts, and let's go!

1 STARTING WITH "WHY"

> *For the first time in history, we are preparing students for a world we cannot clearly define.*
>
> –DAVID WARLICK

~~The world is changing.~~ The world has changed—a lot.

I (Zach) recently went over to my parents' house for our weekly Sunday dinner and witnessed something I never thought I'd see in a million years.

As I walked through the back door, I found my dad lying on the couch, watching...of all things...YouTube.

"Dad? Are you watching YouTube?" I asked.

Even more shocking, he immediately started rattling off all of his favorite YouTubers and channels he's been watching. In his own words, "I can't believe it's taken me so long to figure this out. I've learned more in the last two months watching YouTube than I have in the last two years."

He'd started taking French lessons every night. He had always been a culinary wizard, but now thanks to YouTube, he'd expanded his expertise and learned how to make cheese wheels from scratch and multiple gourmet French pastries (which has added a lot of value to our Sunday dinners).

My dad is not someone I would ever classify as "tech-savvy." I often help him create spreadsheets for his work (hey, now he can learn from YouTube!) But more than anything, this story shows that we are truly living in a new world, a time in which we have access to information at our fingertips and the ability to learn new things quicker and easier than ever before. While this may seem like just a funny story about a man in his sixties discovering YouTube, the reality is that this is the only world our students know. They can't even fathom what life was like before. Soon enough, students will read about what life was like in the B.Y.E. (Before YouTube Era) in textbooks.

We are well aware this message is not new. It is very common to read in education books or hear at education conferences that the world our learners will face will be far different than the world we live in now. We agree, but we also believe an important point is left out—the world has already changed. In the last hundred years, the world has gone through an immense transformation. From candlestick telephones to the iPhone. From writing letters to family to FaceTiming around the world. From silent movies to 8K, 4D, and CGI Animation. From wearing protective goggles while driving to self-driving cars chauffeuring us around! Our current reality is much different than it was even ten years ago. Yet, while schools may have adopted 1:1 technology or brought in carts of expensive tablets, the overall structure and goals of school haven't changed with the times.

The formula for success used to be: Go to school, go to college, get a job, pay your dues, work your way up the corporate ladder, and retire with a fully funded pension and benefits. That simply isn't the norm anymore, and really, this seems more like an exception than the rule these days.

People aren't climbing ladders anymore; they're jumping ships and moving laterally to new companies to grow bigger skill sets. Beyond that, people aren't just jumping ships; people are building their own ships and sailing away. Anyone with an internet connection can work from home, build their own business and start making money (without a college degree or college debt) without ever leaving their (or their parents') basement. If you don't believe us, do a Google search for "Keith Broni Job" and see if his job existed in the early 2000s!

With this shifting reality, schools must redefine themselves to be more than just a launch pad that sends kids off to college. The goal of education must be to prepare students for whatever journey they choose in life. With the current U.S. student debt crisis and the opportunities provided by the widespread availability of the internet, fewer young adults are choosing college as the next step anyway. According to the National Student Clearinghouse, 2019 marked the eighth straight year of declining college enrollments with 231,000 fewer college students than in the fall of 2018.

As teachers, we need to focus on teaching the skills and mindsets that will equip learners for success in life, not just success in school. To borrow and adapt a reference from the late Sir Ken Robinson's TED Talk, "Do Schools Kill Creativity?" kindergartners who are starting school in 2020 will likely be retiring around the year 2080 (Robinson, 2006). We don't know about you, but we can't begin to imagine what the world could look like by then. The question that occupies our minds every day is not, "How do we prepare our students for college?" but instead, "How do we prepare them for the next sixty years of their lives?"

At the start of every school year, during our curriculum night, we begin by asking parents the same question: "Imagine nine years into the future when your kids are finishing their K–12 journey. What do you want for them? What skills, attributes, and dispositions do you hope your students will have as a result of their formal education?"

We have asked this same question at the start of every professional presentation we have given for teachers and have gotten results from well over 2,000 people. Parents and teachers alike are quick to shout out answers like, "independent," "responsible," "motivated," "collaborative," "leaders," "kind," "critical thinkers," and "life-long learners." One hopeful parent even yelled, "out of my basement!" The point of this is that in asking this question, we have never once gotten the answer of "fraction master," "War of 1812 expert," or "someone who knows the difference between parallel and series circuits!"

We have found over and over that when teachers think about their big picture "why," it rarely has to do with the content they teach, but rather the people they want their students to become. So how can we direct our educational efforts to influence the shape and trajectory of the whole learner and not just the student we see before us?

> **WHEN TEACHERS THINK ABOUT THEIR BIG PICTURE "WHY," IT RARELY HAS TO DO WITH THE CONTENT THEY TEACH, BUT RATHER THE PEOPLE THEY WANT THEIR STUDENTS TO BECOME.**
> #ExpertEffectEDU

As teachers, it's our job to use the content we teach to reach *those* skills and attributes that we all aspire to inspire within our students. It's our goal to use our content to unlock the potential within each of our learners. Again, we cannot predict what the world will look like in the future, but we can confidently say that successful people will be the ones who can work on a team, adapt on the fly, think critically and creatively, find and solve novel problems, and always have a willingness to learn and grow. As author Seth Godin says in his 2010 book *Linchpin*, "If you are deliberately trying to create a future that feels safe, you will willfully ignore the future that is likely" ("The two reasons seeing the future is so difficult," para. 3). We need to make our classrooms risk-taking incubators that grow children into learners who are ready for the unpredictable future.

We believe we are living in the midst of an educational revolution—a true turning point for what school can and should be. It's our duty as teachers to raise a generation of learners who have the essential 21st-century skills like critical thinking, collaboration, creativity, and communication to be leaders, doers, thinkers, and makers that will move humanity forward. So let's step out of our comfort zone and break the mold. Let's help create the next generation of movers and shakers that will propel our world forward. Even though we can't clearly define what it will look like, we do believe by fostering these essential skills in schools, we can adequately prepare our youth for this uncertainty. (And hint, it involves way more than just using technology!)

WE BELIEVE WE ARE LIVING IN THE MIDST OF AN EDUCATIONAL REVOLUTION, A TRUE TURNING POINT FOR WHAT SCHOOL CAN AND SHOULD BE.
#ExpertEffectEDU

Here are a few statistics to further our point:

- McKinsey Global Institute estimates that 320 million manufacturing jobs globally will be affected by 3D printing.

- The National Center for Education Statistics reported that in 2015 there were 59,581 computer science graduates in the U.S. with 527,169 open jobs in the field.

Still need more of a reason? Lawmakers are taking notice of the disconnect between the education that a traditional classroom offers with one that can use experts as a learning tool. Recently, states have begun adding requirements to their legislative school code documents, requiring schools to make available in as many fields as practicable opportunities for structured on-the-job learning combined with classroom instruction that enhances students' employability in future careers.

In our home state of Michigan, for example, as of the 2019–2020 school year, districts are to create annual school improvement plans that include specific language and strategies for introducing students to apprenticeships, internships, and other experiences outside of the traditional classroom setting that will help students receive active, direct, and hands-on learning. And that's not all. It is an actual requirement in many states that each school provides students with a variety of age-appropriate career resources so that all learners can complete experiences in a field of interest or aptitude and participate in a follow-up process that provides them with sufficient reflection on those experiences.

Asking our students the age-old question of what they want to be when they grow up is now simply that: age-old—an exercise in futility. Some of the jobs they'll occupy don't yet exist. Other careers they might think they want may be extinct by the time they get there, replaced by robots capable of general artificial intelligence. If we want our students to be employable and prepared for any job, they have to learn how to creatively solve problems, have the learning character to persevere through challenges, collaborate with others, and think critically. In other words, they need to develop the skills and attributes of which robots will never be capable. Every student should have the opportunity to build these skills in their own public school.

To this end, an innovative approach to teaching and learning is required now more than ever. We heard an interesting observation recently that went like this: "You wouldn't set foot into a hospital that practiced medicine in the same way it did fifty years ago, so why on earth would you accept that from a school?"

The most exciting part about this is that the change starts with you. While you might not have the power to change the whole system, you do have the power to be the change in your own classroom.

The idea behind *The Expert Effect* is two-fold. First, students need the chance to be problem solvers, improve their organizational skills, negotiate and compromise, and use teamwork for a real purpose. Connecting learners to real experts in actual careers gives meaning and purpose to what they're learning. "When are we ever going to need to know this?" is not even a consideration when they can see for themselves the real life version of what they're learning in the classroom. And who knows? Somewhere along the way, they may even figure out a better way to do that job. Take Alaina Gassler, for example, a 14-year-old from Pennsylvania who found a solution for automobile blind spots. Not bad for someone who can't even legally drive. Read her story at the link below.

https://www.popularmechanics.com/cars/car-technology/a29668880/eliminate-blind-spot/

Second, connecting students to experts in their immediate community or beyond gives students an important opportunity to learn from people who may possibly look, sound, or believe differently from you and potentially more like them. We, as two white males in our thirties, have a limited number of learners for whom we can serve as mirrors, and we certainly don't want to give off the impression that we are the only knowledgeable experts from whom they can learn. Does it matter? According to a significant body of research, the answer is yes! Students tend to benefit from having teachers who look like them—especially students of color, who now make up more than fifty percent of our country's student population (Miller, 2018). When students are given the opportunity to learn from diverse experts around the world, it shows them *themselves* in positions of power, influence, and expertise.

We have consciously made the effort to reach out to experts around the world who represent the students in front of us better than we ourselves have been able to. This has included beloved authors and illustrators from the LGBTQ community, people of color who were members of the intelligence community from outposts around the world, women in science of diverse faiths, and experts with differing abilities from all walks of life. This diverse exposure, by itself, more than justifies the planning and preparation it takes to bring in members of the global community to serve as expert teachers for our students.

The Expert Effect is more than just three stages to create authentic learning in your classroom; it's about truly rethinking the way things are done in school. It's about giving kids opportunities that will set them up for success for the next sixty years of their lives. We can't wait around for politicians to make changes, for education reform to eek its way through red tape and bureaucracy. The transformational change must start with us, in our *own* classrooms with our *own* students.

WE CAN'T WAIT AROUND FOR POLITICIANS TO MAKE CHANGES...THE CHANGE MUST START WITH US, IN OUR OWN CLASSROOMS WITH OUR OWN STUDENTS.
#ExpertEffectEDU

2 CHANGING THE RULES OF SCHOOL

> *All children start their school careers with sparkling imaginations, fertile minds, and a willingness to take risks with what they think.*

–SIR KEN ROBINSON

I (Zach) didn't love school as a kid. I was the kid who sat in the back of the classroom, hoping I wouldn't get called on. I was the kid thinking in my head, "When am I ever going to need to know this!?!"

At times during my long career as a student from kindergarten through graduate school, I became very frustrated with the feeling that I was constantly "jumping through hoops" to please my teachers in order to pass one class to get to the next. I always explain this feeling when I speak to groups of student-teachers, and I'm afraid someone's head might pop off as the entire audience starts vigorously nodding along in agreement.

Before rewriting the rules of school, it might be helpful to look at how the modern-day education system took root in the first place. According to Dr. Peter Gray in *Psychology Today,*

For hundreds of thousands of years, there were no schools. Kids learned through play and exploration. The first formal schooling started in the colonies, in Massachusetts with the goal of turning students into "good Puritans." As time went on and the world became more industrialized, employers viewed school as a way to prepare people to become good workers. The goal of school was a place to teach compliance. (Gray, 2008)

When looking up the word "compliance" on Dictionary.com, we found words and phrases like,

1. *The act of conforming, acquiescing, or yielding;*
2. *Cooperation or obedience;*
3. *A tendency to yield readily to others, especially in a weak and subservient way*

If you ask any educator why they became a teacher, we are positive you will never hear anyone say, "to get my students to conform," "to create better, more subservient workers," or "help kids become better test-takers." No! As we mentioned before, you'll hear answers like, "to help build a positive future," "to help students become lifelong learners," and "to prepare students to be compassionate leaders in our world." But if we examine the common practices of school: students enter a classroom, sit in their assigned seats, wait for directions from an adult, complete work-sheets or assignments, so they can get a *good enough* grade to move on to the next class or next level...do our actions match our vision? Are we truly preparing students for life or just for the next test?

ARE WE TRULY PREPARING STUDENTS FOR LIFE OR JUST FOR THE NEXT TEST?
#ExpertEffectEDU

Sadly, for many students, learning in school is centered on reading mind-numbing (and outdated) textbook passages and answering follow-up questions at the end of the chapter. We have to admit that since this is what we had grown up doing, it became the way we taught during our first few years of teaching.

Early on, if you had stood outside our classrooms, you might have heard us saying things like, "Walk silently in a straight line on your way to recess," "Do all the odd problems on pages 127–129 in your math book for homework and turn it into *this* basket tomorrow," or "Read each night and document the time and number of pages on this calendar and arrange for your guardian to verify it with their authorization signature!" It would have seemed like not much had changed since the mid-17th century.

As Dr. Gray goes on to say, "With the rise of schooling, people began to think of learning as children's work. The same power-assertive methods that had been used to make children work in fields and factories were quite naturally transferred to the classroom" (Gray, 2008). We have to abandon the idea that modern-day schools are products of logical necessity or scientific insight. As Gray puts so simply, "they are, instead, products of history"(Gray, 2008). We see these historical leftovers as mere compliance tasks, and much of what is done in school today squashes students' willfulness in order to make them good laborers. It goes without saying, but this mentality has serious side effects on students' joy of learning and enthusiasm for school.

May we present to the jury Exhibit A:

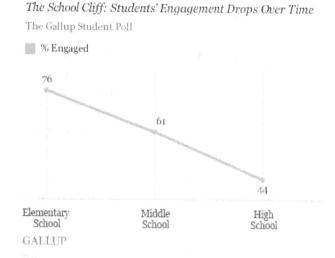

The School Cliff: Students' Engagement Drops Over Time
The Gallup Student Poll

% Engaged

76

61

44

Elementary School   Middle School   High School

GALLUP

Research from a 2013 Gallup Student Poll strongly suggests that the longer learners stay in school, the less engaged they become. In the accompanying article, written by Brandon Busteed, the drop in student engagement is "our monumental, collective national failure" (Busteed, 2013). There are several things that might help to explain why this is happening, but in our minds, it can especially be linked to a general lack of Project-Based Learning opportunities for students as they progress through the corporate-like ladder that is K–12 education...the type of experiential learning that is hard to put a letter grade on but essential for students to learn critical thinking and complex problem-solving skills.

The traditional goals of the educational system as we know them—reading, writing, and 'rithmetic—are no longer the in-demand skills that students need for the future. Instead, the outlook of what's most needed for the next generation are skills like creativity and originality, analytical thinking and innovation, leadership, and social influence. Of course, these skills are still important, and we're not saying to throw out every textbook or worksheet and don't teach essay writing, but there must be opportunities in school for kids to go deeper than this. We must give our students time to explore their passions and participate in exciting learning opportunities that grow these skills organically.

Our world no longer rewards people who are just good listeners and memorizers; our world rewards people who can take what they know and apply it to unique situations. Our world no longer rewards compliant workers who can do one task really well; our world needs makers, doers, innovators, and game-changers! It's time we stop teaching the YouTube Generation for an assembly line world.

IT'S TIME WE STOP TEACHING THE YOUTUBE GENERATION FOR AN ASSEMBLY LINE WORLD.
#ExpertEffectEDU

It's not about what we say we want to do or mean to do as teachers. It's about making our actions align with our vision to create true and lasting change. Yes, our job is to teach the curriculum and the content standards, but we get to be creative with *how* we teach every day. Our goal is to use the content to develop the kind of learners with a hunger and thirst for learning long after they leave our classrooms. We want to see learners who are asking their own questions rather than asking us if their answers are correct. If we want children to be passionately engaged in learning, we must give students a sense of ownership over their work. We must get students to buy into what they're doing in school, so it doesn't feel boring, meaningless, worthless...and mere compliance.

Yes, there are times we all need to be compliant in life (the IRS, student loan servicers, and mortgage companies are not very flexible with their deadlines), but there are also times when we need to step out, be bold, and try to solve problems in creative ways.

So, let's rewrite the rules to the game of school!

Schools need to allow learners to see the purpose of their learning and guide them towards careers that will interest them, as well as prepare them for their future. Using the framework we will lay out in *The Expert Effect,* you can be the one to make this shift towards preparing students for the unknown future no matter where and what you teach.

In this book, we hope to give you an outline, a framework, and a new mindset for teaching and learning. (Notice we don't simply say "schooling" because education and schooling are unfortunately not always the same thing!) We're not saying to throw out all direct instruction or to stop doing everything you do. We want to challenge you to reexamine your practices, dream big, be bold, and take action to create memorable learning experiences for your students. Exchange that mindset of 1930 for 2080. Reimagine your classroom and see where you can swap out compliance for creativity.

3 YOU ARE AN EXPERT, TOO!

> *We are all experts in our own little niches.*
>
> –ALEX TREBEK

Congratulations! If no one has told you this yet today, we're here to tell you that you (yes, you) are an expert!

Since we started the journey of writing this book and traveling around presenting on this topic, we've heard many questions and even some pushback about the word "expert" and its meaning. While writing this book, we saw multiple questions posed on Twitter asking the question, is it even possible to become an expert in education since there is always more to learn?

Let's be real here. It's impossible to be an expert on every single aspect of teaching (and if there's anyone claiming that they are an expert on *everything*, run, hide...be very wary of them!). As teachers, we wear a million and one different hats and serve in as many different roles. You almost certainly are good at most of them, outstanding in some, and have room to grow in others. We feel this especially as elementary teachers, since we teach every academic subject area for our students. Expertise is a continuum. That's the beauty of teaching; there's always someone who will know more than you and that you can learn from, but we also all have our own areas of expertise from which we can teach others.

It's time that we recognize teachers as experts. Think about all the training sessions, multiple degrees, copious amounts of professional development, countless hours spent reading professionally, and voluntary Twitter discussions that teachers take part in while "off the clock." This profession receives too much negativity in the media, and it's time that we own the fact that we are experts in our own right, making an incalculable positive impact on the greater society.

In reading many articles with snazzy titles like "There Are No Experts," or "There's No Such Thing as an Expert," it seems the negativity surrounding the word "expert" stems from people self-proclaiming their expertise to get you to buy their product for "three easy payments of $19.99" like a snake-oil salesman. By nature, teachers are some of the most humble people on the planet and often feel uncomfortable selling themselves in this way. But, we're not selling snake oil; we're preparing the youth of today for the future. If we want more respect for this profession, we must be proud and share the awesome things we are doing. Say it with us, say it loud, and say it proud: *We are teachers, and we are experts!*

You are the expert in your classroom. You are the expert of your students. You are the expert of your curriculum. There's no consultant, author, or speaker who is better at gauging your learners and what they need than YOU. Being an expert doesn't mean you've reached the finish line of your career or arrived at a place where you're finished learning. Experts make mistakes too, but what sets them apart from the rest is the willingness and ability to change based on self-reflection. What makes someone a true "expert" in our eyes is their relentless pursuit to improve. If you're holding this book right now, we know you are in the pursuit of greatness for the sake of your students. When you learn, grow, and improve your practice, your students are the direct beneficiaries of your growth.

We're here to show you that you don't need to be the ONLY expert in your classroom any longer! You can take the pressure off of yourself of needing to be the be-all and end-all resource for your students. When we create opportunities for students to connect with outside experts, we expose kids to the content in a new and real way which can supercharge the learning process.

Can you even imagine if late-night talk shows never had any special guests? Or what television news broadcasts, newspaper articles, or public radio programs would be like if the only person you ever heard from was the anchor or author? It couldn't be considered as objective news anymore—it would be opinion journalism at its best, and mere assertion or propaganda at its worst—boring, one-sided, and very unreliable. Professional journalists count on the expertise of insiders to give their reporting credibility and gravitas. Without consulting outside experts, our society would lose a pillar of truth and dignity. One time, while interviewing a journalist about the writing process, a student in our classroom asked, "What's the most important quality for a journalist to have?" The answer? Integrity and credibility. We believe that providing your classroom with the same type of resources that news organizations depend on, and taking them through the process of learning from experts, you will be helping your students to see that there is an infinite supply of information in the world—and that acquiring knowledge and other perspectives doesn't have to stem from a classroom teacher-centric approach.

There's a very famous notion that can be loosely attributed to a fellow Michigander, Henry Ford, that goes something like this, "Smart leaders surround themselves with smarter people." This doesn't happen by accident. It happens because of the leader's self-awareness in their own strengths and weaknesses. It happens because they're confident enough to say, "I don't know, but let's find out together." Later in this book, we'll talk more about why this is especially important to do in front of your students, but for now, let's pause to think about pulling in outside experts to create powerful learning opportunities for your students.

We feel as though students deserve to learn from the best, and we know you do too. When we elevate learners to the level of experts in the field, we show them that they are worthy of learning from experts who are living the learning every day, and we show them that they are worthy of similar accomplishments. We show them that we believe that *they* could be *them* someday. It's a validating gesture and one that goes a long way towards making students own their *own* education.

Please don't mistake our message. We are NOT saying that to enhance your students' learning, you must find the number one, world-renowned expert in the desired field of study. You just need to find someone who knows more than you (and most of all, who's good at connecting with kids). We want to find people who live the work daily and can provide real-life context for your students' current area of study. So, we're here to redefine what an expert means for our context (and oh, do we love acronyms!).

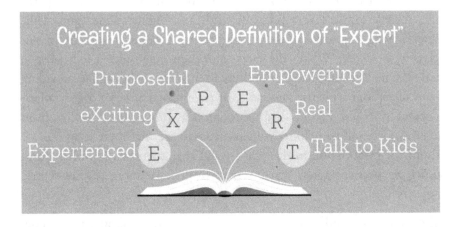

Let's take a look at this a little closer. We want to connect our learners with people who are:

Experienced: As the 1922 Nobel Prize winner Niels Bohr famously said, "An expert is someone who has made all the mistakes which can be made, in a narrow field." The difference between an expert and an amateur is the expert has dedicated their life to their field and made all the mistakes to learn all the lessons. We want our learners to hear from the people who have made mistakes and learned from them, not some "self-proclaimed, know-it-all, perfect guru."

eXciting: Yes, we had to cheat on this one a little for the X factor, but we want someone passionate about what they do. Passion is contagious. No matter what subject, if we have a passionate expert, kids will get excited too, creating a positive effect on the entire learning process.

Purposeful: We do not want you connecting your students with experts just for the sake of doing it; it must be purposeful to the content in your classroom. Since you are the expert on your curriculum, you can pick the wellsprings into which you'll dive—the areas of your curriculum in which you can make a purposeful connection with an expert that will deepen student learning. We don't have time to do this with every subject, so choose wisely and dive in!

Empowering: The purpose of connecting students to experts is for them to see a new perspective on a subject. We want them to dream big and go after what they want in life. Connecting them with experts empowers them to keep the dream alive or create a new vision for their future.

Real: This is simple. If we're learning about the weather, we want to connect our learners with someone who lives and breathes that daily. We want the experts to have real-life experience to talk about and uncover the relevance.

Talk to Kids: It's great if we connect kids to world-class experts, but if they talk in only academic language geared towards adults, it will be pointless, painful, and even have an adverse effect! We must find people who can speak on a level your children can understand, relate to, and learn from.

This book is about giving students access to multiple experts who can supplement what the expert teacher in the classroom is already doing. Being a teacher is like being a Michelin Star chef, and giving your students access to real-life experts along with high-quality instruction is like adding the perfect blend of spices to that finely cut filet mignon.

4 LAYING THE GROUNDWORK FOR SUCCESS

Culture eats strategy for breakfast, lunch, and dinner.

–PETER DRUCKER

It would be easy for us to make the claim that you can make a greater instructional impact by sprinkling in a few Zoom calls with experts here and there, but we all know it must go deeper than that. To create true, transformational learning experiences, we must first work to create a classroom culture that values deep thinking, creativity, and one that inspires students to believe that their learning actually matters by finding ways for them to share their work with the world. When we teamed up to co-teach, we wanted the biggest shift to come from the culture and expectations we created for thinking and creating in the classroom. We had to ask ourselves, as all teachers must, whether we wanted to create a culture that promoted deep learning or a culture that perpetuated the game of school. A positive, non-threatening atmosphere where students felt able to speak up, offer ideas, and take risks without fear of reprisal or mockery—or a classroom focused on perfection, standardization, and uniformity. We dubbed our class The 4th-Grade Innovators to take that "innovator's mentality" and make it a core part of our culture every single day of the year.

When we think back to our years as students, we can both remember those teachers in whose classes we loved being and other classes in which we felt anxious and uncomfortable. (Try feeling at ease in an art class after being hoisted a foot in the air by your belt loop for whispering to a second-grade neighbor during a drawing demonstration.) What was the difference between the two? The answer is simple: the presence or lack of a positive classroom culture.

You can be the most fundamentally sound, pedagogically gifted teacher, but if you fail to intentionally create a classroom culture where students know their input is valued and risks are encouraged, the learning will suffer. Neither of us will ever claim to be pedagogically gifted as teachers, but we do take pride in creating a strong culture within our classrooms by putting forth a deliberate effort to promote this kind of thinking and educational buy-in from students. This work starts on the first day of school and lasts all year long.

One way to set your students up for success is by explicitly stating your classroom values up front. In the past, my (Zach's) classroom rules were very straightforward and teacher-driven...à la Harry Wong. *I* would spend the first days of the school year going over all *my* rules (boooooor-ing), and then we (oh wait no, *I*) would create a poster for the wall on which students would sign their life away (and then never really refer back to again). My early classroom rules were something along the lines of:

1. Safety first;
2. Always raise your hand to speak or ask a question;
3. Be respectful to all adults and students;
4. Be responsible for your belongings;
5. Only one student in the bathroom at a time;

...and so on and so forth...

But just before the 2017–18 school year, while browsing through Twitter, I saw a tweet from Amy Fast (@fastcrayon) that inspired me to change how I was going to start the school year.

Amy Fast, Ed.D.
@fastcrayon

Classroom rules:
1. Have a vision.
2. Be a learner, not a finisher.
3. Lean into struggle.
4. Feed your passion.
5. Own your education.

After seeing that tweet, I made it my goal to let students have ownership over the rules in our classroom. During the first week of school, each student got a pad of sticky notes and was to write out every rule they thought we needed for our classroom. By the end of this, we had about 120 colorful stickies papering the walls. As a class, we then sorted all of these ideas into major categories and came up with the following five rules for our classroom that we could actually live by:

1. Start each day with a positive vision.
2. Learning is messy, embrace the process!
3. Always choose kindness.
4. Step out of your comfort zone.
5. Strive to make the world a better place!

When Zach sent me that first tweet and his class's version of the vision soon after, it spurred me to make a change as well. What my fifth graders had referred to previously as the "Kindergarten Rules" (things that even the youngest of learners come to take for granted) were thrown out the window. Not another second would be wasted on nagging kids to clean up their desk spaces, or debating who had to go to the bathroom most urgently under the "only one person in the bathroom at a time" policy. We would instead turn our energies towards striving to make the world a better place. These weren't just rules, they were expectations for learning, and we made it a point to live into these expectations every day.

Another burst of inspiration came from reading David Geurin's (@DavidGeurin) eye-opening book, *Future Driven: Will Your Students Thrive in an Unpredictable World?* After finishing this book, I was inspired to not only adopt the moniker of The 5th-Grade Futurists for our class, but to also establish a mission statement for our learning. Again, instead of choosing a cutesy nickname for our class, affixing it to a bulletin board, and never thinking of it again, I wanted our classroom's theme to be a living, vibrant influence on the culture of our class—in this case, helping to guide our learners on a meaningful mission. I wanted to help students develop transferable skills that would help them be happy and successful no matter what their own future looked like...ready to empathize, be engaged citizens, seek justice, and to be upstanders, not bystanders (Geurin, 2017, p. 8). As a class, we brainstormed, generated, and sorted through ideas of how we could do that from within the confines of our classroom. The result became our classroom mission statement and helped to set the course for everything that was to follow. In this chapter focused on laying the groundwork for success, we thought it would be appropriate to leave you with what we established for ourselves:

I CAN USE MY LEARNING TO IMPROVE MY OWN LIFE
I CAN USE MY LEARNING TO IMPROVE THE LIVES OF OTHERS
I CAN USE MY LEARNING TO IMPROVE THE WORLD AROUND ME

Does your classroom have its own mission statement? Are the rules of your classroom aligned to your vision for learning? These might be helpful questions to consider when beginning the year or laying a strong enough foundation to make deep learning a reality all year long.

The difference we noticed between this method of involving students and their ideas and the old teacher-driven method of forced compliance was that we actually referred back to these rules—or expectations for learning—daily. They were the lens through which we could understand the importance of our learning. And if a connection couldn't be made, then that in itself was a strong indicator that it was maybe time to move on to doing something more meaningful. These expectations shifted the culture in the classroom and set high expectations for learning and for ourselves. It sounds simple, but it made a world of difference.

Another of our favorite ways to create and maintain a strong classroom culture is by leading a daily morning meeting. This is one thing we do every single day, even throughout the distance learning during the 2020 Coronavirus pandemic while in-person classes were suspended. We do it because we know it makes a big impact on the culture in our classrooms. We set the goal to start each day with a positive vision, so we literally take thirty seconds at the beginning of our morning meetings to close our eyes and create a positive vision for the day. In sports, before any game, coaches give a pregame speech and go over any last-minute plans or strategies right before game time. This is how we view the morning meeting in the classroom. It's a pep talk to start the day off with a positive intentionality and provide students with some inspiration and wisdom for the day.

Throughout the year, we cycle through different themes like Carol Dweck's Growth Mindset, positive energy/self-talk, the power of positive habits and choices, goal-setting, mindfulness, gratitude, and making a positive impact on the world. We have discussions about meaningful quotes, read an inspiring picture book or two, and watch inspiring videos that teach life lessons. When we focus on things that teach our children how to be better people and not just better students, they see that we care for them on a deeper, holistic level. (Read much more about morning meeting methods at zachrondot.com/morningmeeting.)

The conversations and discussions we have during our morning meetings might not directly relate to reading, writing, math, science, or social studies, yet it promotes a culture of positivity in our classroom. Because we spend fifteen minutes on this every single day, it shows that we value their personal growth as well as their academic growth. During this time, it's always especially rewarding for students to talk about times they were able to step out of their comfort zones to try something new. Giving students the opportunity to take a risk by sharing in this low-stakes environment not only helps them understand the importance of living into the positivity of our classroom culture, but also grows the courage required to take on the challenge of public speaking when teaching others as experts (more about this in Part III).

One of the most gratifying feelings as a teacher is when former students come back to visit. I (Zach) always show them their class picture on the wall and then ask the question, "What do you remember from fourth grade?" This may come as a surprise, but no student has ever said, "the Unit 8 math test" or "that time we read about the Toledo War." Typically, students tell me that they remember the different projects we did, big activities or field trips we went on, the books we read together, or the fun facts and wise words from our morning meetings.

In true serendipity, as I was writing this chapter of the book, I got a note in my mailbox at school that was mailed to me from a seventh-grade student I had had three years prior. In her note, she wrote, "I will never forget how you never gave up on me. I still remember the wise words quotes and how you would talk about *the power of yet*. I remember how you always said, 'You miss 100% of the shots you never take.'" This simple note reminded me that when kids think back on my class, they don't remember the times I failed while taking a risk as a teacher, or the lessons that weren't perfectly executed (trust me, there were plenty). Children will remember the way we made them feel when they were in our classrooms. To me, this is what culture is all about: when your students know you care about them as a person more than just their score on a test, the learning process becomes significantly more powerful.

The culture in any classroom is also in part a result of the tasks on which the teacher puts emphasis and value on. If we told our students that we want them to be innovators and world-changers, but then filled their day with rote memorization activities and multiple-choice worksheets, the culture would match our actions, not our vision. We have both spent a lot of time poring over our curricular unit calendars to figure out the areas into which we can dive down the rabbit hole to create meaningful and authentic learning opportunities for our students. These are the projects on which we expend the most time and energy and are a reflection of the values we hold as teachers and of our classrooms' cultures.

In the last section of this book, we break down some of the many big projects we have done with our students and how we have leveraged the three-part *Expert Effect* System to achieve these awesome results. We have given students opportunities to create their own mock-businesses, create app prototypes that would make the world a better place, write letters to local and state-level politicians, create podcasts that have been listened to world-wide, and more. Yes, we still do worksheets (occasionally). Yes, we still write perfectly formatted essays (frequently). But when we take the time to do big, meaningful projects and put students' work out into the world, we set the groundwork for deep learning and create powerful cultures in our classrooms that children appreciate and remember.

Some may say, "My curriculum is so dense, there's too much to cover to make time for this kind of thing daily." And we get it. As educators today, it seems like we are constantly being given new curriculum, new initiatives, and new challenges to the point where we can't take ONE...MORE...THING! This is where we both put up our shields and fight to protect the activities and projects we know will benefit our learners in the long run.

We are absolutely not saying to throw everything away or ignore your curriculum, but we challenge you to take stock of what kinds of tasks you are devoting time in your classroom. We challenge you to seek out those in-depth investigations into which you can dive headfirst and create magical learning experiences with your students. These are the things children will remember...and help create your legacy as a teacher in the process. Please trust us when we say that the return on investment you get from building a strong culture—whether through a morning meeting, positive visioning, or simply creating student-driven agreements for the class—is more than lucrative.

INTRODUCTION: THINK + TWEET

#ExpertEffectEDU

1. What skills should we, as educators, put the most emphasis on to prepare students for careers that don't yet exist and an uncertain future?
2. In what ways can we work with students to begin shaping the future now?
3. What is an ExPERT, and how can tapping into one improve your educational outcomes for your learners?
4. What can you do to create a strong classroom culture intentionally?
5. Think back to being a student. Which teachers' classrooms did you enjoy being in? Which ones did you not? How did the teachers make you feel? This is a huge indicator of classroom culture.
6. What might go into your own classroom mission statement?

PART I

LEARN FROM EXPERTS, NEAR AND FAR

5 LEARNING FROM EXPERTS

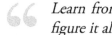

Learn from the experts; you will not live long enough to figure it all out by yourself.

–BRIAN TRACY

When we were in elementary school, we thought our teachers were the smartest people on the planet. And there was no question—they were the smartest people in the classroom. They were the holders of all the knowledge, responsible for transferring it to us, the students. Schools were the necessary centers for learning. That's where the teachers were. That's where the libraries were, with all the books to learn from! However, this formula has changed. No longer are we, as teachers, the smartest people in the room. It's not even close because...

Google beats us every time.
YouTube knows how to do more things than we do.
Siri is faster than we are.
Alexa is more convenient.

NO LONGER ARE WE, AS TEACHERS, THE SMARTEST PEOPLE IN THE ROOM. IT'S NOT EVEN CLOSE...AND THAT'S OKAY!
#ExpertEffectEDU

While this can seem threatening, we believe this also provides incredible learning opportunities for our students. No longer do we need to feel the pressure to know the specific ins-and-outs of every subject we teach. We were just discussing this recently after listening to a teacher share how they are just barely learning certain science topics before the students do, and how they hate it when they cannot answer their class' questions. It's okay to look at this as a learning experience, and it is okay not to know the answer. Students will learn more if *they* have to figure it out, or at least brainstorm the sources they could use to find the answers. We now have unlimited resources at our fingertips to help teach learners the content, and part of our new job description *should be* to help students learn how to find the information for themselves.

Now, now…don't feel too bad about this.

Teachers still (and always will) play an *essential* role in the classroom and in the learning experiences of their students. Our jobs will never be farmed out to a robot (the COVID-19 Pandemic has made this clearer than ever). Our jobs, however, are evolving.

Whether our students end up forging a career as Drone Air Traffic Controllers, App Developers, entrepreneurs, or employees of a company, there are certain skills that only we can teach that will give our learners the best opportunity for success in life, regardless of the path they choose. After all, preparing young people for success should always be the ultimate goal of education! Whatever the future of each student will look like, we need to prepare them in the best possible way. So what might innovative education look like over the next decade? To us, innovation happens through the cultivation of new relationships with real experts out in the world from whom our students can learn. Who better to share insights and experiences about real-world applications of their learning than the people who have dedicated their lives to the field?

AS TEACHERS, OUR ROLE HAS CHANGED FROM THE STOREHOUSE OF KNOWLEDGE TO THE FACILITATOR OF LEARNING.
#ExpertEffectEDU

As teachers, our role has changed from the storehouse of knowledge to the facilitator of learning...like a talent agent putting our "clients" in touch with the right people at the right time. One of our favorite ways to facilitate this learning is by connecting students with real-life experts in the field related to what we are studying. British author and speaker, the late Sir Ken Robinson (2015) puts it so well in his book, *Creative Schools: The Grassroots Revolution That's Transforming Education*:

> *What's being made possible now, with the digital technologies as they're evolving, is a whole process of self-directed learning that has never been available before. Now you can go online, you can get all this stuff for yourself. You can get online, connect to people from all over the world. Join a massive open, online course (MOOC), taught by the best people in their fields, for next to nothing.* (Robinson, 2015, 2:26:36)

Whenever starting a new unit, we immediately start to ask, "Who can we connect our students to help deepen the learning?" and thanks to technology, these experts don't even need to be geographically convenient for us! Skype, Zoom, or any other video conferencing app are all amazingly convenient ways to connect with people, near and far. There are so many benefits to be had when you invite an outside expert to share the responsibility of educating your students! Here's the shortlist:

1. Students are exposed to a wide diversity of ideas, careers, and professionals
2. Students realize the importance of education and skills needed in every job/career
3. Students gain experience using interview skills

4. Students to hear and see information presented in a novel way through various modes of technology

5. Students find answers to their wonderings from primary and expert sources

When our fourth graders studied extreme weather during a non-fiction research and informational writing unit, our teaching partner, Mrs. Amanda Oliver (@Mrs_AOliver), reached out to local Meteorologist Kevin Jeanes and asked if he would Skype with her class. Instead, he asked if he could come into our school and speak to all the 4th graders directly! As you can imagine, this was way more engaging than the teacher standing at the front of the classroom trying to explain the role of a meteorologist. As an added bonus, he even put the class' pictures on the local news the next morning! You should have seen their faces as they walked in the next day, having seen themselves on the news. Same effect as reading from a textbook? Not even close.

In the same unit of study, another parent reached out to share that one of Grayson's students had an aunt who worked for The Weather Channel in Atlanta and was more than willing to Skype in to provide a full tour of their studio. We spent an hour virtually touring the studio, learning how green screens worked, how computer modeling helped make accurate weather predictions, and having students ask specific weather-related questions related to their area of study.

When my (Zach) class decided to start The 4th-Grade Innovators Podcast (more about this in Part IV), neither I nor the students had any idea how to start a podcast. I reached out to Kelly Croy, host of the Wired Educator Podcast. He graciously Skyped with us to teach us about the art of podcasting. He taught us about using a dramatic and engaging voice, not to worry about the number of views and likes your podcast gets, and instead focus on putting out good content to the world. This was a valuable experience for all of us, and every time we created a new episode, we referred back to Kelly's advice.

When learning about the tourism industry in Michigan, I emailed a variety of people who worked on the famous Pure Michigan advertising campaign. After a few attempts, someone from the team Skyped to share all about the campaign and taught us valuable information about Michigan's tourism industry that we never could have learned from our outdated Michigan history textbook.

When our students were learning about entrepreneurship, Grayson reached out to our favorite educational entrepreneurs, the creators of the Flipgrid video discussion experience, to have them share about their entrepreneurial journey. They Skyped with our fourth-grade classes who had gathered together in the gym and were able to share what it truly means to be an entrepreneur and start your own company. Neither of us would have been capable of sharing this information because we're teachers, not entrepreneurs!

The wonderful thing about finding experts to which you can connect your students is that it takes some of the pressure off of you! You don't have to pretend to be an expert at something you're not. You can find an expert willing to talk to your students and share their knowledge. Students won't remember every science lecture or language lesson you put together, but they will remember the time they were (virtually) hanging out in a penguin colony in Antarctica or chatting with someone who just rowed a boat across the ocean—and you can make that happen for them!

The well-known education researcher and New Zealand professor, John Hattie, has added further confirmation to this conclusion in his 2015 report, *What Works Best in Education: The Politics of Collaborative Expertise.* He concludes, "The greatest influence on student progression in learning is having highly expert, inspired and passionate teachers and school leaders working together to maximize the effect of their teaching on all students in their care" (p. 2). To us, this means not only being an expert teacher yourself (you are), but also surrounding ourselves and our learners with the smartest people possible—those "high experts" with knowledge and skills from within our own community or beyond, relevant to whatever the task at hand demands.

The teacher's expertise comes into play during the brokering and brainstorming stage and also in preparing students for the interview with your community expert. Teaching about questioning techniques, what's appropriate to ask and what isn't (kids seem to always want to ask about how much money someone makes), and how to create a record of learning are all part of the classroom teacher's role. And the work doesn't end when you hang up the phone (not that we really "hang" up phones anymore). The teacher is essential to help process all the new information they just received. The power of this type of experiential learning comes from the debrief and discussions afterward that continue throughout the entire unit. Without a teacher to help them, students trying to make sense of an "expert experience" is like children trying to drink from a fire hose of information. The teacher is the guide on the side who can help them separate, organize, and distill the information to help learners delve into the complexities involved in directing one's own learning for understanding. The teacher also works to craft the important messages from the experience into the lessons that follow to ensure it's not just a "one and done."

Tips to Find Experts

So now that you're ready to connect your learners with experts, let us give you our best tips to do so. If students are asking, "When am I ever going to need to know this stuff?" and you don't have a good answer for them, you've already lost the battle. We need to provide them with meaningful and relevant learning experiences and then allow learners to have the chance to make their mark. We get to do that! Part of that hope can come from learning from people around the world and seeing the different perspectives that are out there. Virtual field trips or collaborations can help your class connect academically and emotionally, giving them the chance to see exactly "when they're going to need to know this stuff."

Before we give you the goods, we need to offer a disclaimer. As we've already stated, times have changed—a lot. Even as we write these words, the world continues to change right in front of our eyes. Just the other day, we received an email from one of our top resources we use to find expert-classroom connections. They revealed that their platform was evolving, and that we should be prepared to find the kind of experiences we'd come to expect somewhere else. This was a huge blow

—to lose one of our most trusted sources of outside expertise. However, it shouldn't have been unexpected. Change, after all, is constant.

With this in mind, some of the sources below that we suggest may merge, transform, or cease to exist entirely over the course of the next ten years. Instead of relying entirely on our list of go-tos, we suggest you have your own general checklist of look-fors when scouting out new methods and communities you can use to form global connections for your class. Remember the EXPERT acronym?

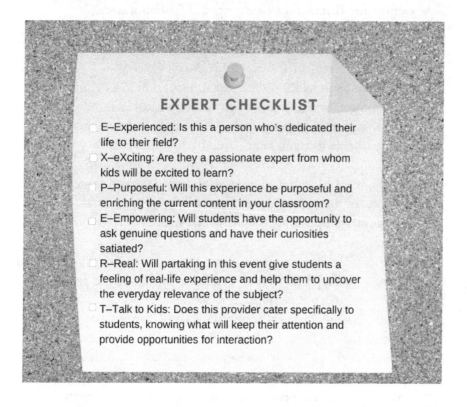

EXPERT CHECKLIST

- E–Experienced: Is this a person who's dedicated their life to their field?
- X–eXciting: Are they a passionate expert from whom kids will be excited to learn?
- P–Purposeful: Will this experience be purposeful and enriching the current content in your classroom?
- E–Empowering: Will students have the opportunity to ask genuine questions and have their curiosities satiated?
- R–Real: Will partaking in this event give students a feeling of real-life experience and help them to uncover the everyday relevance of the subject?
- T–Talk to Kids: Does this provider cater specifically to students, knowing what will keep their attention and provide opportunities for interaction?

If the answer to these questions is mostly yes, then you're good to go! It's important to vet your sources by talking to them beforehand, dropping in on another event they've scheduled, reading other teachers' reviews of them on Twitter or other networks, or reading testimonials on the provider's website. Your students' ability to glean meaning and significance from these opportunities can't be overstated, so let's elevate student learning and get them connected!

1. Research Different Learning Hubs: In order to find experts in the field that you think would be willing to connect with your students, learning hubs provide a great first place to look. There are tons of great resources for live and interactive sessions out there. Here we'll share some of our favorite organizations that make connecting with experts super easy:

- **Center for Interactive Learning and Collaboration (@cilcorg):** The Center for Interactive Learning and Collaboration, or CILC for short, makes learning from experts extremely convenient and accessible. Much of their programming provides an understanding of different cultures and heritages, bringing new awareness to student learning. Their live, interactive programs are inherently inclusive and bring participants to museums around the world that they would not otherwise be able to visit. Programs we've used through them have ranged from being free to be paid content. You can also sign up for a weekly newsletter to get constant updates about upcoming programs that may be of relevance to your classroom.

- **Skype a Scientist (@SkypeScientist):** The mission of Skype a Scientist is simple, yet impactful: to make science accessible and fun through personal connections with scientists. Skype a Scientist has created a database of thousands of scientists and helps them connect with teachers and classrooms worldwide, making science education available and engaging for everyone. Giving students the opportunity to get to know a real scientist and get the answers to their personal questions is incredibly valuable. Furthermore, it shows the importance of researching using primary sources. When you sign up to be connected with a scientist through this website, their foundational values are clear—inclusion, diversity, and honesty. When submitting a request for an expert connection, they ask for your preferences as to what kind of role model you'd like your students to learn from—not only what type of scientist, but also what gender, ethnicity, faith, and so on—in order to try to match classrooms of marginalized students with scientists from the same group for improved representation. Mind blown!

- **The Pulitzer Center (@pulitzercenter):** Want to inspire your students with global issues and the journalists who cover them? The Pulitzer Center is committed to building global awareness through education. They work with elementary schools, high schools, and universities to bring pressing international issues into the classroom through in-person and Skype visits, and even include lesson plans to help make the most of the expert experience. Our classes have connected with nationally recognized and award-winning female journalists who have given us tips on our writing and interviewing skills. It's amazing to be talking to these experts via Skype one day and to hear them on the radio or read an article they've written on the internet the next.

- **Exploring by the Seat of Your Pants (@EBTSOYP):** Exploring by the Seat events bring the excitement and educational value of learning by connecting your classroom with scientists, explorers, and conservationists from all over the world who are working to protect ecosystems as well as the incredible biodiversity found within. Using technology to broadcast live into classrooms from the most remote regions on the planet, this hub makes science education and conservation adventurous and exciting. Learning about weather? Try Zooming with a meteorologist on Mount Everest. Learning about endangered species? Drop in on a live Q&A with guest speakers from the Lewa Lion Conservancy in Kenya. And the best part of all? It is and always will be free for classrooms everywhere!

- **Microsoft's Flipgrid (@Flipgrid):** In recent years, Flipgrid has continued to evolve and grow to do an even better job of being a fully-integratable digital feature of classrooms' learning systems. Their Disco Library (short for Discovery) is chock-full of fascinating and engaging topics, added by both expert content providers and other teachers from around the world. Students can watch short videos that stimulate curiosity and spark discussion, then students can respond with their own thoughts, all within a safe online learning environment. Utilizing Flipgrid's ever-expanding file of topics and fun video editing features can turn even the most reluctant student into an expert commentator and content producer. Even as we write this, Flipgrid has just launched a new lineup of virtual field trips on which classes can embark. This will no doubt turn out to be one of our go-to resources moving forward, with the added bonus of being able to allow students to reflect on their experience directly within the already useful app.

- **Discovery Education (@DiscoveryEd):** Discovery Education is another great resource for finding live and pre-recorded virtual field trips. We have used this resource for great experiences like celebrating International Dot Day, inspired by the book by Peter Reynolds, Computer Science Week, and specific virtual field trips relating to our social studies curriculum. One caveat to this resource is that you need an account to access many of these experiences. We are both lucky that our school district has provided us with accounts to take advantage of these great resources. If you have access, this is another great place to start.

2. Curate a List of Individual Organizations: Through our own trial and error with the above-mentioned learning hubs, we have found some of the most experienced content experts to lead our class through engaging inquiry. Build your own reliable list of experts that check off what you're looking for. Some of our own most-trusted sources include:

- **California State Parks System (@portsprogram):** The California State Parks PORTS Program offers free interactive virtual field trips for K-12 students to stay connected to the region's natural, cultural, and historical resources. Connecting your classroom to California State Parks allows your students to learn and explore with professional docents working in public parks across the state. Memorable trips we've taken include visiting the Calaveras Big Trees State Park to learn about giant sequoia ecology, as well as traveling virtually to the Columbia State Historic Park to learn about the history of human interaction with the environment during the California Gold Rush era. Check with your own state or around your region to see if there are similar virtual learning options available.

- **Michigan Science Center (@mi_sci):** MiSci's ECHO distance learning program brings live science demonstrations and activities directly to your students over the internet. Whether your class is learning in-seat or remote, you'll surely be able to find something to meet your students' needs. While most of their programs have a fee associated with scheduling a point-to-point session, they also have a phenomenal (and free) YouTube channel, where many of their programs are live-streamed and allow you and your students to participate in interactive and fun learning in real time or after the fact at your convenience.

- **The Smithsonian Institutions (@smithsonian):** We've had several experiences videoconferencing with presenters from the Smithsonian who show artworks from America and around the world from the museum's many collections. Through inquiry-based questioning and discussion, presenters engage with participants as they explore artworks together, using thinking routines to better understand the cultural significance of the pieces presented.

- **Buffalo Bill Center of the West (@centerofthewest):** The Buffalo Bill Center of the West is the educational gem of Wyoming. Their expert interpreters provide interactive student-centered virtual field trips on all things related to the wonders of Yellowstone National Park, the adventurous lives of mountain men, the rich cultures of Plains Indians, and more.

- **National World War II Museum (@WWIImuseum):** The National WWII Museum engages with learners from all across the world through a variety of distance learning programs to connect students with WWII history and honor the generation who sacrificed so much to secure our freedom. Programs include a broad range of topics, allowing students to learn significant stories from Pearl Harbor to D-Day without having to make the trek to New Orleans, where the museum is located.

3. Just Ask: Sending a simple short email explaining that you are a teacher looking to connect your learners with experts can have a lot of power. It can be scary to ask seemingly random strangers, but guess what, we have something special to offer them: kids! Everyone wants to help kids (especially in the business world...it's great PR for them!)

Here's a sample email I sent to a member of Michigan's Department of Tourism who later Skyped with my class:

4. Dream Big! It's truly priceless when you see the look on a student's face who is having a conversation with someone they never dreamed they would be talking to. Famous authors, local celebrities, presidents of companies...the more we talk up these people and build up the excitement, the more powerful the experience becomes. Reach out to these people and just see what they say. The worst thing that can happen is you hear nothing back, or receive a regretful "no," and the best thing that could happen is they are thrilled to get your request and want an excuse to step out of the office for a few! Occasionally, they'll pass along your request to someone else in the organization who would be more able to assist you, and that's a win too! These are the experiences kids run home telling their parents about and the ones that make a lasting impression on them.

5. Build a Diverse Coalition of Experts: As we mentioned earlier in the book, you, as the classroom teacher, are an expert in knowing your students. What are their interests, needs, backgrounds, beliefs? When searching for outside experts with whom to connect them, you are uniquely situated by virtue of your position to seek experts that will not only speak to them, but will *speak* to them as role models. Exposing your students to diversity of all kinds is valuable because avoiding homogeneity improves teaching and learning. Children enrich their ability to think critically and creatively as they engage in conversations across differences, especially when all learners' cultures, races, religions, are reflected and embraced.

6. Don't Let Rejection Get You Down: We have both sent many emails or requests that didn't get a response or get a rejection, and that's okay! We recognize that people are busy, and it's not personal. Just find someone else and keep asking for help. As we said, many people will go out of their way to help teachers and students out!

7. Test the Tech: Once you have set something up, make sure to test the technology you are going to use with the actual person before to make sure everything will go smoothly. I can't tell you how many times I have set something up, and the volume or connection wasn't strong enough and wouldn't work. There's nothing worse than trying to troubleshoot the technology with impatient students and an expert on the other end waiting for you. Set up a time on the day of the event before students arrive or on your prep time to make sure everything is good to go. You'll be glad you did!

8. Take Note of Time Zones: Be sure to know what time zone the person you are trying to connect with is located in. One of our first-ever experiences with having an expert speak to our class ended up more chaotic than it needed to be because we realized we were an hour off due to neglecting the time-zone difference. It worked out in the end though, it was just an added lesson for our students in adapting to change and going with the flow.

6   FIELD TRIPS "IRL" (IN REAL LIFE)

> *No, no, ain't nothing like the real thing, baby*
>
> *Ain't nothing like the real thing.*

–MARVIN GAYE & TAMMI TERRELL

In case these lyrics don't hammer home the point, we'll say it again. There's nothing like the real-life, in-person experience of learning about something directly from the source, at the source. Field trips in real life meet that need. Think about it. When you were growing up, what were some of the most impactful memories of your time in school? For me (Grayson), it was hands-down those field trip experiences. Well, to be perfectly honest, it may have just been the bus ride to and from our destination (and I think that's still partly true for kids today).

I vividly remember a field trip in eighth grade, in which we took a charter bus on a week-long tour of the east coast of the United States. We traveled through Canada, so we could stop and see Niagara Falls (from the good side) and rode the Maid of the Mist boat tour at the bottom of the drop. Our first night was spent at a hotel in Binghamton, New York, and we spent the next morning exploring "The Big Apple."

We took a walk through Central and Battery Parks and had our first experience with haggling over some Oakley sunglasses and fake Rolex watches with some local "entrepreneurs." We toured Washington, D.C., Mt. Vernon, and Madame Tussaud's. We explored the Smithsonian Museums, took a tram through Arlington Cemetery, then traveled on to Gettysburg where we learned what it was like to be a civilian during the infamous battle. I had the time of my life riding rides at Hersheypark in Pennsylvania, and afterward, we reboarded our motorcoach to head for home. Arriving back in West Michigan, I was a changed person. The memories created from this experience as a student are ones I still think about to this day.

Perhaps it was this experience that helped spark the desire for adventure in my young self, as I would later go on to study abroad twice and travel as often as possible while attending Western Michigan University (go Broncos!). From Canada's annual Shakespeare Festival to supplement my English minor, to Boston for an alternative Winter Break experience volunteering in food banks and toy drives for children. From visiting Chicago's Art Institute with the Lee Honors College to living with a host family in Spain, and traveling on to Ireland, England, Germany, France, Switzerland, Italy, and the Netherlands. Once you catch travel fever, the only prescription is more travel—so you might as well expose your students to it as early as possible!

If we were to rely solely on our district-provided Michigan social studies textbook, Jennifer Granholm would be the current governor, which, at the time of writing this, is already three administrations and five terms of office behind the times. That's probably as close to real-time as textbooks go, too! Think of the last time your district adopted a brand new curriculum. This happens maybe once or twice in a teacher's career? With dated information and values, the textbook is clearly not current or engaging enough to do an adequate job of teaching our students what's important about our home state. Enter the field trip...IRL!

Every year we turn to the real-life experience that field trips offer to bring our content to life and make it engaging. To us, true learning is meaningful learning that sticks with learners long after they leave our classrooms. We would be doing the next generation a great disservice if all we did was get them to memorize dates and facts from the text and fill in the bubbles on the end-of-chapter test. To achieve this goal, we don't rely on just one experience to make the learning stick. We look to as many as our school's budget will allow.

Obviously, you don't want to hear about every field trip we've taken over the past two decades of our careers, so for the sake of brevity and clarity, we'll give you one year's worth of trips on the big yellow busses that all helped our students dive into learning about their home state of Michigan. To give you an example from our own classrooms of using field trips in real life to give our students the chance to learn from experts, we'll take you into the "fascinating" realm of Michigan's state history, from the time of the first ice ages to the present-day (or thereabouts).

Some of the "deep dives" on which we've taken our students include The Michigan History Museum in Lansing, which presents them with an overview of our state's history. Next, we took them to The Detroit Historical Museum, located in the city's Cultural Center and Historic District of Midtown. There, we learned the chronicles of history of the area from cobblestone streets, 19th-century stores, the auto assembly line, 17th-century fur trading, and much more.

Of course, one must save the best example for last, and our field trip to Mackinac Island and Historic Mill Creek was our pièce de résistance. At the start of the 2016–2017 school year, we asked the question, "What if the sky was the limit and we were able to teach Michigan social studies in the best way conceivable?" By the way, this question shouldn't be far-fetched or outlandishly absurd. After all, our students deserve to become experts by learning from experts. Why not expect the best for all students? We answered our own question by saying it would be great to give our children the chance to visit the national landmark of Mackinac Island, a small island rich in history off the coast of Michigan's upper peninsula...frozen in time. No cars. No chain restaurants. Just horse-drawn carriages, bicycles, historic forts, the iconic Grand Hotel, and it didn't hurt that we'd be able to stock up on the world-famous Mackinac Island Fudge while we were there either.

On a brisk May morning, 45 students, 40 parents, two teachers, and one principal loaded up on two busses at 4:30 AM to embark on a 36-hour learning excursion that took us five hours into beautiful northern Michigan. We first spent our time roaming the island on foot and by bicycle and toured Fort Mackinac (the oldest still-standing structure in the state), which was used during the War of 1812. Later, in nearby Mackinaw City, we toured a sawmill established in the late 1700s and ended our day doing what all Michiganders should do after a long day of learning: roasting marshmallows over a campfire on the shores of Lake Huron.

For some, it was the first trip away from home without their parents. For others, it was the first time they had ridden a bicycle. For all, it was the first time they had operated a full-scale and operational water-powered sawmill. For none was it a waste of time or another "boring" day of sitting in a classroom. Students were living in history, drinking it in 360 degrees with no wifi required. Field trips remain a favorite method for providing students with authentic learning opportunities. The power of this field trip continued when we returned back to the classroom to dive deeper into the historical topics that we just saw in real life. These topics were no longer just pictures and words in a book, they were places around which they had walked and had seen with their own eyes.

I'd like to share one quick story that has little to do with giving your students an authentic environment in which to learn, so I hope you'll indulge my digression. At the time of our first trip to Mackinac, I (Grayson) had been in the midst of an interview process for an open elementary principal position within our district. When they had called me earlier in the week to schedule the day of my interview, I realized that I would be out of town—out of the lower peninsula—at the time of the scheduled meeting. I asked if I could possibly do the interview over the phone since I would be unable to return from the island on my own and leave the group behind. They acquiesced. As our tour group of fourth-graders was leaving the parade grounds of historic Fort Mackinac to head up to the ramparts to witness a live-fire exercise of their 18th-century canons, I got the call...perfect timing. I excused myself from my teaching partners to answer the phone, and I was greeted by the interview committee through the speaker of my phone. As we began with the pleasantries, a cannon exploded in the background, sending billowing clouds of smoke over the hillside and towards the bay of Mackinac. Between the soldiers calling out signals to reload the cannon and the booming of light arms and heavy artillery, it was a tad difficult to focus on answering questions about the role data plays in school-wide decision making, but it was certainly a meaningful learning experience for the students gathered round in awe of the firepower. Needless to say, I did not get the job, but it certainly made for one of the most memorable interviews of my career.

In taking these trips, we are giving our learners, and even in some cases their families. These memories will last a lifetime and definitely will be applicable on the next assessment, high stakes or otherwise. Field trips for fun to the cider mill or the pumpkin patch certainly have their place in making students enjoy learning, getting parents involved, and helping to build a community for your class, but they lack the depth of content that curriculum-specific field trips can provide.

We strive to make our curriculum a living, breathing, and, most importantly, constantly changing document, and we think you should too. No one should ever tell you, "We teach what's in the textbook." We urge you to constantly question your curriculum. Ask yourself, your department, or your grade level team, "Where is the best place for this lesson to be learned?" The classroom may not always be the best answer. But can an environment still be considered authentic and beneficial to learning if it is completed in a classroom or on campus? Yes, we think so! "Authentic" does not necessarily have to mean "real," but instead could simply be a realistic task in your traditional academic setting. As long as you avoid propagating decontextualized memorization and instead challenge students to think and solve problems just as professionals would in the real world, you can still claim that stamp of authentic approval.

One quick story about a time when our classroom turned out to be the perfect place for a lesson—we were learning about magnets and how one of their applications included using the Earth's own magnetic field to aid in navigation via the compass. We handed out compasses along with a treasure map and ushered our fourth graders out our back door. For about ten minutes, teams traipsed around our playground and athletic field, following directions like, "forty paces north," and "twenty paces east." The directions, which we had roughly guestimated just a few minutes before, would eventually lead learners directly back to where they had started...our back door. Their indignation about having been led on a wild goose chase quickly evaporated. Behind the door was hidden a big box of popsicles, and teams who successfully navigated their way back to our classroom were rewarded with the sweet treat. On that occasion, the classroom and school grounds turned out to be a perfect fit for our purposes! Field trips don't need to be multi-day and expensive excursions...sometimes they can be just that—a trip to a nearby field!

The key to selecting and planning these experiences is finding a foothold or tie-in to your existing curriculum. What concepts or standards are particularly difficult for students to grasp? What subject seems to merely have its surface scratched by the materials you currently have? Field trips in real life just can't be beat for offering a depth of knowledge that's unmatched in authenticity, excitement, and relevance for kids.

7 IN-SCHOOL EXPERIENCES

> *Better to see something once than hear about it a thousand times.*
>
> –ASIAN PROVERB

Between the logistics of setting up field trips months in advance, the management it takes to collect permission slips, and the financial aspect of it...it's just not realistic to do too many of these throughout the year. So, to combat the challenge of overcoming the costs of bringing learners to the locale but still provide our students with enriching learning opportunities, we like to find as many relevant experiences as we can to bring the expert to us at school. Just as the old adage "a rising tide lifts all boats" is associated with the idea that an improved economy will benefit all citizens, we believe giving all of our students a shared in-school experience will benefit the educational outcomes for all. Here are a few of our personal examples of turning in-school experiences into memorable learning opportunities.

Lumberjack Day

As we mentioned, in fourth grade, our social studies curriculum covers the history of our state from the most recent ice age up until about yesterday. As you can imagine, learning about 15 thousand years in 180 school days can be quite a challenge. One way to more effectively teach this is to take a big chunk of time and create an entire day's experience out of it. Our favorite example of this is "Lumberjack Day."

We have a friendly local lumberjack named Sheepshank Sam who comes to school and puts on a full-day lumberjack experience for our students. Kids dress up in their best lumberjack attire, which includes overalls, steel-toed boots, rugged flannel shirts borrowed from dad's closet, and beards smeared on with face paint (or black and brown markers from our classroom when those who come in clean-shaven realize they're missing out). This all helps to make it a fun experience.

The first part of our day includes Sheepshank expertly blowing on his Gabriel's Horn to sound the start of learning. This would normally have been done to wake up the lumberjack camp, but in our elementary school gymnasium, it has an equally stimulating effect! Students first learn about the daily life of a lumberjack via an old-timey slideshow with actual slides (this is a whole other lesson for learners who have never seen such a device). Next, Sam brings out a massive trailer full of lumberjack equipment to show students different saws, clamps, drills, sledges, and more before asking for volunteers to act out various lumber camp roles. The kids trip over themselves to be picked so that they can wield what look like 19th-century torture devices. They learn who lumber barons, river hogs, cookies, fallers, and gandy dancers were. They sit on the deacon seat, hear why there was no talking allowed in the mess hall, and learn why one would never want to eat "macaroni." If any of these terms are confusing, then clearly, you could have used Sheepshank's in-school experience and not just your textbooks.

For lunch, we have a traditional lumberjack feast with pancakes, bacon, eggs, sausages, and much more to fuel up for an afternoon of lumberjack work. This is a wonderful opportunity to get parents involved by flipping pancakes and pouring orange juice, but even more importantly, it gets them into the school to see the meaningful learning in which their children are engaging in person. Finally, in the afternoon, our outdoor school field is divided into three different stations for students to act out the jobs of lumberjacks. They saw logs, heave timber, and pay artistic tribute to the white pines of Michigan.

This day is a truly immersive learning experience. We could spend weeks reading from the textbook, memorizing dates, and taking a test to see what was memorized, but nothing can compare to students holding the tools in their hands and physically carrying out the tasks of a lumberjack.

The Native American Experience

Part of our fifth-grade curriculum in Michigan involves learning about the Native American cultural regions of the United States. Our textbooks give this aspect of our country's history a cursory glance at best and doesn't come close to bringing the culturally-rich heritage of these Indigenous Nations to life for our learners. It can be a challenge to get students excited and engaged while reading about our nation's first people since it may at first seem so far removed from their current lives. This is an important topic, and we want to honor their cultures—both historic and present-day— by going bigger with it, so we needed to call in an expert to guide us and bring these distinctly beautiful cultures to life.

Enter Mr. Gary Ghareeb of The Native American Experience. He, unlike our texts, is able to reach out to students by verbally, visually, and tactilely engaging them. His passion comes through with every story he tells, and he's able to help students see the meaning and importance behind the history and the legends of the people. He spends hours setting up his presentation in our media center, carefully laying out animal skins, hand-made tools, weapons and armor made of bone and wood, beaded jewelry, and feathered headdresses on tables, organizing them by tribe and time period. He sets up games that Native people played, and after explaining about them, actually lets the learners play. The day is a perfect blend of explanation and hands-on experience that easily keeps fifty fifth graders engaged and entertained.

Mr. Ghareeb is the perfect illustration of what can happen to student understanding when in-school experiences are employed. Many aspects of early Native American life are explained thoroughly and backed up with authentic artifacts, and you could really tell that the students were interested and captivated. When people like him have been dedicating their whole lives to collecting and making the items that students need to see and feel in order to grasp what it was actually like to be there, a more memorable learning experience is made. If going to an actual Native American museum or cultural center is not an option, whether due to lack of funding, transportation, or time, bringing in an expert to help teach your students can give them the chance to learn in a way that does the subject matter some semblance of justice.

At the beginning of the 2020–2021 school year, during a time that usually is filled with the scent of new school supplies and fun first days of getting-to-know-you activities, our school district instead was forced to begin the year virtually due to the global pandemic. Our Native American unit of study is usually one of the first we undertake, but because of the social distancing precautions, we knew we wouldn't be able to have Mr. Ghareeb back inside our school. However, this regional treasure was able to come through for us in a big way, and none of his exuberant enthusiasm for the modern Native American cultures of North America was lost in translation through Zoom! Kids were spellbound by his energetic expertise on our virtual field trip, in which he expertly wove together professional-quality video clips of his collection and explanations with time for questions and answers. When you find a source like this who can meet the needs of your students no matter what, hang on to them. You've hit the jackpot!

Sidenote: While I (Zach) did not teach this unit, this example helped me make a connection to a conference I attended abroad last summer. I had the opportunity to travel to Australia to attend the World Congress on Positive Psychology, and one thing I noticed right away was that every session started by the speaker acknowledging and appreciating the land and the Indigenous Peoples who were there long before us. This was consistent in the schools I visited, the conference, and also in the many places I traveled to on my own across Australia after the conference. It made me wonder how their education system teaches students about their first people compared to how the subject is taught in the states. In any case, bringing in an expert in this situation was one way to elevate the importance of the subject and pay the topic the respect it was due.

Science Alive and The Living Tidepool

These two in-school expert experiences show how science can literally come to life when you get the right people involved. This first, Science Alive, comes from a local company that brings animals to your school (no doubt, there are numerous companies doing this exact same thing in your neck of the woods). Their furry friends range in species variety from the cute and cuddly to the downright disgusting. We've seen them bring in chinchillas, toads, sloths, and snakes, but they offer other programs where animals such as hissing cockroaches and tarantulas can come into play too. Now, we ask you, is there any reason more definitive than this to invite experts into your school? In this way, you will never in your life have to deal with cockroaches and tarantulas! You can leave it for an outside expert to handle!

The second company, The Living Tidepool, brings the experience of exploring these rocky pools filled with seawater that occur at low tides in the ocean to your school. Now, being from Michigan, we know marine ecosystems. We are literally surrounded by the water of the Great Lakes on almost every side, but oceans we do not have. Made possible through the development of mobile aquarium tanks, this group brings their live animals to you along with informational presentations and programs. The traveling creatures our students were able to literally get their hands on included hermit crabs, sea stars, sea cucumbers, sea urchins, anemones, keyhole limpets, sea snails, mussels, scallops, algae, and more!

When it comes to deciding between reading about these creatures in a book, watching a video about them, or physically reaching out and touching them with your hand, it's a no-brainer. Inviting engaging experts into your school is clearly the more formative learning experience when paired with your own expert ability to help students prepare for and process what they're learning about.

8 DISTANCE LEARNING

 We need to bring learning to people instead of people to
learning.

—ELLIOT MASIE

When we originally wrote this chapter of the book, the idea of
distance learning was nothing more than a distant thought. But
then 2020 came along and the whole world was turned upside down due
to the COVID-19 Pandemic. The best way I (Zach) can describe this
extreme shift was that on March 6th, 2020, I gave a presentation to a
group of student teachers at Central Michigan University called "Ten
Truths for Teaching with Technology." During this full day of presenting, I never once mentioned the idea of teaching our students entirely
online from home; it had never even crossed my mind. On March 12th,
our governor announced all school buildings would be closed down for
the safety of staff and students (at the time for three weeks, which then
turned into the rest of the school year). Just six days after that presentation, distance learning was our reality.

As always, educators did what educators do—quickly shifting gears to
pivot in order to provide the best education possible for students during

this "emergency remote learning" situation. This was a difficult transition for educators and students alike. As teachers around the world worked to uproot and overhaul an entire system overnight, we set out to put our own *Expert Effect* system to the test.

During those first few weeks, we were both completely overwhelmed by all the companies and individuals who stepped forward to provide free resources to support crisis-learning. It was hard to sort through them all. There were tons of low-quality materials out there. We were not interested in the "free worksheet" type of offers that flooded the internet and our inboxes, but there were a lot of other really high-quality resources to be found if you knew where to look.

Amazing authors like Kelly Yang (@kellyyanghk) took to Instagram and recorded free webinars to teach students about the writing process. Kwame Alexander (@kwamealexander) read from his own award-winning *Rebound* to keep young people connected to choice literature by listening to his fluent, flowing readings. Illustrators like Jarrett Krosoczka (@StudioJJK) and Mo Willems (@The_Pigeon) offered daily drawing classes that kept students engaged in art from home. Emily Arrow (@helloemilyarrow on Instagram) provided us with the most endearing music and story classes from her place in Portland. Through Facebook Live, the Cincinnati Zoo (among others) had their zookeepers giving live, daily animal talks on the most amazing species. Local yoga studios and athletic trainers around the world stepped up and gave homebound children (and adults) free daily workouts to keep minds and bodies going strong.

These are the types of events we look for that fit perfectly with our *Expert Effect* system: high-quality distance learning that allows students to learn directly from the experts in their respected fields. We were incredibly grateful for these people who made their crafts accessible to us from our homes because in some regards, this period of crisis learning was one of the most enriching parts of the school year for our students. We weren't trying to recreate what had always been done at school in a virtual format. Rather, we were looking for and taking advantage of some of the most novel and engaging educational solutions to a global crisis. Despite that fact, we are NOT hoping for more self-quarantine any time soon! Instead, sending students on virtual field trips to learn from experts near and far can become the norm in your classroom! It shouldn't take a pandemic to bring out the creative learning opportunities!

When the pandemic closed our classroom, I (Grayson) was in the middle of teaching a fifth-grade reading and writing unit about the time period of American history known as Westward Expansion, the 19th-century movement of settlers heading to the American West which began with the Louisiana Purchase and was fueled by the Gold Rush, the Oregon Trail, and a belief in "Manifest Destiny." Students were finishing up their research into topics that would soon make up the chapters of their own self-made textbooks.

One day prior to sending students home for the last time, we had partaken in a virtual field trip to a California boomtown to learn about the Gold Rush. When the mandatory closure came, we had no closure of our own on the subject. We had to find a way to wrap up the weeks of hard work we had already put into this ongoing project. Three final expert encounters were still scheduled on our calendar, as students had expressed a desire to learn more about the transcontinental railroad, the mistreatment of Native Americans during the time period, and the Oregon Trail. Luckily, the expert presenters from the Smithsonian Institute in Washington, D.C., and the knowledgeable docents at the Durham Museum in Omaha, Nebraska that we had coordinated with were up to attempting to teach our students remotely from their own homes. We signed on to Zoom as a class, and just like that, we were all back together again, picking up from where we had left off and finished gathering information for our research. It was a much-needed dose of normalcy amid those unprecedented times.

Studies show that virtual field trips can raise interest and motivation for students and help students have a more positive attitude towards their learning. In a study completed by Mary Oyler from Northwest Missouri State University, students with learning disabilities who participated in a virtual field trip showed over 20% growth in subject comprehension and over 10% growth in vocabulary for that subject compared to students learning with traditional methods (Oyler, 2014). We believe that having access to these types of experiences in school will increase school-children's interest, knowledge, and motivation towards learning.

The type of experiential learning we attempt to give our students is linked with theories of constructivism that introduce the belief that learning is an internal process whereby children construct knowledge by integrating experiences through a process of assimilation and accommodation, building and refining concepts as new information is required (McRainey & Russick 2010; Yardley et al. 2012). In short, providing your students with as many opportunities as possible to immerse themselves in a learning experience, guided by an expert, will work to even the playing field, offering students who may be disadvantaged to form connections and gain experiences that would otherwise not be possible.

Imagine you wanted to know who the first person to reach the South Pole was...you Google it or simply ask Siri, right? You find out that it was a man named Roald Amundsen. Maybe you even receive that tidbit with a little extra factoid: he was an explorer (duh) from Norway. Great. Thanks. Google does an excellent job of telling you exactly what you want to know, and not an ounce more. That's how Google works. Its algorithms for returning information to a query is based on what other people are also reading. There's nothing new...nothing novel. However, we believe there's a lot of information that you can understand even better when given facts along with more context. Learning facts without context means they don't have anything to connect to—they just flow in one ear and fly out the other. Virtual learning experiences help deliver the same information you'd get in a web search, plus the all-important context which makes the learning stick.

I can tell you that Amundsen was the first to reach the South Pole, and it matters. But when I put you amongst the ice, in a deadly race to the bottom of the world, it's a different discussion. In 1910, two teams of men wanted to go to the South Pole. One team was from the United Kingdom. The team was led by Robert Falcon Scott, a Royal Navy officer. The other team from Norway was led by Roald Amundsen. Both men wanted to reach the South Pole first. No human had ever reached that location before. That sort of contextualizing experience is afforded by distance learning opportunities when you discuss the subject with the people who have made it their life's work to know all there is to know, the people who read the footnotes and found out what Amundsen liked to put on his toast in the morning (by the way, it was fresh seal, sled dogs, and penguin meat).

Distance learning opportunities are much more feasible than real-life field trips, and research backs up their effectiveness. In a control-based study in the 2003–2004 school year published by eSchool News, 400 seventh and eighth graders went through the experience of three virtual field trips. The findings were that these students scored higher on national reading comprehension tests than students who used traditional learning methods alone. Throughout the article Suzanne Clewell, faculty member at Johns Hopkins University states, these online field trips are most effective when they come with targeted instructional support materials that can help teachers and engage students. Clewell goes on to say, "If they don't have the support of the teacher, [students] are not going to succeed" (Clewell, 2005 as cited in eSchool News).

Also, let us repeat, this study was done in 2004. Technology has come so far since then, and it's so much easier to take students on virtual field trips now than it was back then. By utilizing platforms like Skype, Zoom (yes, we used Zoom before it was "cool"), FaceTime and the like, we can connect our students with outside experts through face-to-face calls, virtual field trips, or webinars and help to slow and close the gap of experiential knowledge that may exist.

Virtual Field Trips

One great use of technology is to create authentic learning experiences for students via virtual field trips. Virtual learning programs help to close the opportunity gap for students. Whereas regular field trips have obvious geographical constraints, virtual field trips shatter that limitation by allowing you to take your students *virtually* anywhere (pun intended.) When studying World War II during a historical fiction reading unit, we "took" our students to the National World War II Museum in New Orleans (a cool 1,074 miles from our school!) A museum employee walked around the museum while talking to us through Skype, showed us the exhibits, and told us stories. Students were sitting on the floor with their notebooks fully engaged and learning. With the emergence of virtual reality and augmented reality, we can only imagine the world of virtual field trips will continue to become more powerful. Back in Chapter 5, we shared some of our own personal favorite providers of distance learning opportunities, but we would encourage you to search for other museums, historical societies, or educational institutions that might offer other programs specifically tailored towards what you're looking for. They are easy to schedule and include no bus requisition forms, permission slips, or anxiety over lost children!

Webinars

Webinars are typically less intimate than Skyping with an expert or taking a private virtual field trip because there are hundreds of other classes tuning in as well, but the purpose and outcome can still be the same. These distance learning opportunities are usually free and open to all educators. By finding these through simple internet searches and pre-registering with some basic information, most providers will allow you to watch the webinars live or recorded on YouTube. Some interesting and engaging ones we've attended with our students were provided by educational technology organizations like Newsela, code.org, and Girls Who Code.

During National Computer Science Week, our favorite educational technology company, Seesaw, did a series of webinars to promote computer science skills and careers to students. The web designers and the creators of Seesaw walked us through the six essential steps to creating an app. This was a powerful learning opportunity that we certainly could not have taught our students (never having created an app ourselves). During these webinars, there is usually a textbox for chatting to type questions to the presenters. When our class got our questions read and answered out loud, it only added to the excitement of the experience!

Virtual Reality Possibilities

I (Zach) recently attended a conference on providing global experiences for youth in schools. I attended a session on virtual reality, and the possibilities blew my mind. With simple equipment like a smartphone and a wide variety of Google Cardboard viewers to choose from under $20, students can literally be transported around the world. While sitting in the session to plan for our upcoming unit of study, I searched: "Earthquake 360 Video" on YouTube, clicked the option to "Watch in VR", put my phone in the Google Cardboard goggles, and was instantly standing in the middle of an earthquake. For teachers like us in Michigan, who (luckily) don't experience earthquakes, this gives our students the opportunity to learn by being immersed in the danger while standing safely in our classrooms.

My mind started racing with possibilities. We read a book each year which references the ceiling of the Sistine Chapel in Vatican City, so I searched "Sistine Chapel 360." In moments, I was standing on the floor of the Sistine Chapel staring all around at the beautiful ceiling from 4,600 miles away. Have a student who wants to be a surgeon? Search "Surgeon 360 video," and they can be standing on the floor next to surgeons performing actual surgery! With this technology, we now live in a world where we don't have to physically travel somewhere to be there.

The above examples are as simple as using YouTube to search "360 videos," but there are other apps worth exploring like Google Expeditions, which allows students to explore the world with over 1,000 locations preloaded to explore. You can travel to cities across the world and virtually walk down the streets.

We won't sit here and pretend like this is the same experience as actually being in the middle of an earthquake, at the Sistine Chapel, or in the middle of an operating room, but is it better than just reading about it in a book? Worlds better (pun intended)! These technologies are just getting started. It is crazy to think about how much better these will get over the next ten years and what impact it could have on education. These are ways you can truly bring your content to life and allow students to explore what they're studying and see it with their own eyes.

Between all these different types of point-to-point virtual programs (and based on a very rough estimation), our students "traveled" about 24,000 miles in the 2018–2019 school year alone. This estimate is on the low end of the spectrum if you were to only make one virtual field trip per month during the school year. Skype sessions with sea life conservatories, offices of technology start-ups, museums of natural history, science centers, authors' writing retreats, and zoological societies are available at the click of a button, and dramatically increase students' worldly awareness, building the all-important schema from which they increase their knowledge base.

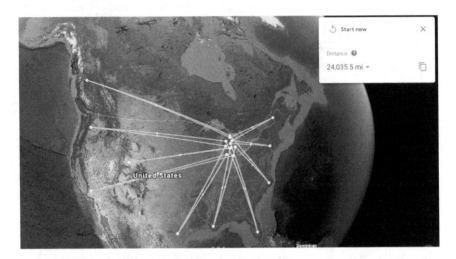

Using the strategies we outline in *The Expert Effect*, you can explore different scenarios and make them more illustrative. Our younger generation needs interactivity to really understand and contextualize the issues that we're facing. We, as humans, take care mainly of our personal and immediate problems. When you are able to make it personal, you create a space for empathy in the hearts of your students. We need to do everything we can to stop the spread of knowledge differentials between the "information haves" and the "information have-nots." It is our belief that providing students with frequent, easy, and relatively inexpensive experiences through these distance learning events will help level the playing field for students and give them global connections around the world.

9 TIPS ON TALKING WITH EXPERTS

> *Always the beautiful answer who asks a more beautiful question.*
>
> —E. E. CUMMINGS

In the same way that a reporter or biographer needs to do their preparatory work before an interview, students also need to be prepared to talk to and learn from experts near and far. This in itself is a skill that needs to be taught and practiced, because many children don't have the experience of speaking with adults in an academic setting. Similarly, it's sometimes the case that the expert is not used to interacting with children, which can make matters even worse. We've seen these events fall apart at the seams with students lying down on the floor, getting up in the middle of the conversation and walking away, or simply being rude with their questions and not actively listening to answers. It's not pretty. Sometimes experts will talk above students' levels, and the children will sit in a bewildered stupor, unintentionally sending signals of boredom, and that's just not what you want either. Practice and preparation can help mitigate situations that waste the expert's time, and more importantly—that of your students! Before you set up your first opportunity to have students learning from an expert, we highly recommend spending time talking about these tips and practicing them beforehand, perhaps with another teacher, parent, or principal. This is another example of "setting the groundwork for success."

Before the Expert Experience:

When you arrange a meeting with an expert, we recommend you have your students generate some of their questions in advance. Questions that begin with "who," "what," "when," and "where" typically provide answers that are more narrow in scope and shallow in complexity. While sometimes these questions are necessary for clarification purposes, we recommend trying to ask questions that start with "why" or "how" in order to create the most generative questions possible. These types of probing questions often lead to the most interesting answers and longer explanations. It's okay to have a mix, especially when students really want to know something (despite the non-generative nature of the query), but highlighting this difference is an important skill for students just learning the art of the interview. Find below some sample question starters:

- Why is it important to...?
- How would it be different if...?
- What are the reasons for...?
- Suppose that...?
- What if we knew...?
- What is the purpose of...?
- How would _____ change if...?

Every time we've talked with experts in the field, whether it's with a paleontologist out in the field in Colorado, an entomologist in a lab in Illinois, or an author/illustrator in our own school library, these professionals always comment on the caliber of questions that students ask. We have gotten comments like, "Your fourth-graders were asking questions like the high schoolers I just met with last week!" Questioning deeply and imaginatively can help us identify and solve problems, come up with novel ideas, and pursue research from fresh angles. Helping students to form a more beautiful question truly does result in a more beautiful answer, and so much more.

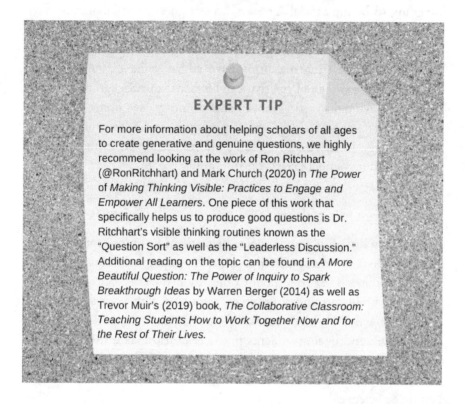

EXPERT TIP

For more information about helping scholars of all ages to create generative and genuine questions, we highly recommend looking at the work of Ron Ritchhart (@RonRitchhart) and Mark Church (2020) in *The Power of Making Thinking Visible: Practices to Engage and Empower All Learners*. One piece of this work that specifically helps us to produce good questions is Dr. Ritchhart's visible thinking routines known as the "Question Sort" as well as the "Leaderless Discussion." Additional reading on the topic can be found in *A More Beautiful Question: The Power of Inquiry to Spark Breakthrough Ideas* by Warren Berger (2014) as well as Trevor Muir's (2019) book, *The Collaborative Classroom: Teaching Students How to Work Together Now and for the Rest of Their Lives.*

Finally, don't forget to set a tone of excitement before learning from that outside expert. We like to really pump students up by saying things like, "You won't want to miss Friday. We're talking to an expert who can help to answer some of the lingering questions we've had about_____!" This gets the kids thinking about the topic outside of the designated time to learn about it; it encourages discussion at home with their families about what they're learning in school. Plus, it shows them how excited you are for the experience, thus demonstrating the attitude of a lifelong learner!

During the Expert Experience

To start things off, it always helps us to choose one or two students who are going to be the official "greeters" to our guest or collaborating classroom. As an added bonus, it's always better to not have to look at your own LED-lit face staring back at you through the webcam (although recently, video chatting platforms have added some digital reimaging features, such as one in Skype that can blur out your background, conveniently removing distracting movements or messy classrooms, or the one in Zoom that can "touch up" your appearance and adjust for less-than-ideal lighting). In any case, we strongly recommend you create a script to make sure the experience starts off smoothly.

Sample Script for Students

Creating a script with your students helps them feel more confident and prepares them for the experience. Also, it might help those who feel anxious about talking to an adult other than their teacher. Preparing a script and brainstorming appropriate responses with your students can be good practice for their speaking and listening skills. By creating a script before and having students practice, it also makes this experience feel like a big deal. Here's an example of how one fifth-grader introduced our classroom to an actual paleontologist from the Denver Museum of Nature & Science:

Student Script

Hello! Good morning, my name is Olivia, and this is our class, The 5th-Grade Futurists from Troy, Michigan. We have been learning all about Earth's various systems, such as the biosphere, the atmosphere, the geosphere, and the hydrosphere. We are very excited to talk with you today about your recent fossil discovery in Colorado and ask some questions about how the K–Pg Asteroid Impact affected these different systems around the world. Please feel free to start by telling us a little bit about yourself and where in the world you are.

Managing All the Questions

You might be wondering, "What about all of those questions that we generated before the expert experience? How do you manage that?" After having our class participate in Skype conversations a few times, we realized that there is an art to administering all of the questions that students had generated, making sure each student was prepared to ask their question, and avoiding a lag in the conversation. Here are some of our best tips to help make the most of your experience.

One approach we found very useful was to have all of the student questions typed out into a Google Slide deck. While using our mobile Skype cart on wheels to speak directly to our guest speaker (more on this in Chapter 10), I (Grayson) would project the slides onto the SMART Board. In this way, they were able to look into the camera, see the expert on the TV screen, and behind that would be their question, acting like a teleprompter. This left their hands free to hold a microphone that ran through our classroom audio system, and they didn't have to fumble with notecards or notebooks. After one student's question had been asked, I would advance the slide for the next student to see that they were "on deck," allowing them to come forward to the screen and get ready for their question. While the first questioner would stand and listen to the response to their question, I would often see the one up next mouthing the words to their upcoming question. This oral rehearsal would help them prepare like an actor waiting in the wings, and when they were "on stage," they would introduce themselves and ask away.

This setup is only feasible if you happen to have multiple screens and multiple devices, which we realize not everyone does. Chart paper would work just as well but would require flipping the pages every so often (which could be a student job). It also only works if you are the only group of students asking the questions. The difference between point-to-point and multi-point webinars is based on the ratio of classrooms to experts. In a point-to-point experience, there is one expert and one classroom learning. In a multi-point setup, there may be multiple classrooms around the world learning from one expert synchronously. In these types of situations, your class may be limited to asking only a handful of questions on camera, or may only be able to ask questions through the chat box feature of the video call/webinar. More information on the variations between platforms and the different types of calls is outlined in Chapter 8.

Allow the Expert a Preview of the Questions

If you're participating in a point-to-point conversation, it may be helpful to your expert to have a preview of the questions ahead of time. Sending the questions to experts in advance can help them prepare for the questions your class will ask, and it also helps you keep the guest from revealing answers to upcoming questions prematurely! For example, if an expert is introducing themselves or talking about their work, they may inadvertently give away some information that a student was slated to ask them. This is an unfortunate occurrence because it can kind of take the wind out of a student's sails. If they're all prepared to ask their great question and then the guest says the answer without even being asked, it's like someone else blowing out your birthday candles. Not fun! Sending them the questions in advance can give them a heads-up as to what's to come, and may help keep them from revealing "spoiler" answers.

Additionally, giving your expert a preview of the questions helps them to plan how they'll spend their time with you. Do they normally give a half-hour presentation and only leave five minutes for questions? Do they prefer to have their guest appearances flow more conversationally? Giving them your questions in advance can be helpful for their planning purposes, and I (Grayson) know firsthand that visiting experts appreciate the practice. Chad Sell (@chadsell01), author and illustrator of the graphic novel *Doodleville* and other beautiful works for children, let me know how impressed he was with the time we had put into our planning: "I appreciated how much thought and preparation you did last year with your students in preparing questions about *The Cardboard Kingdom* after reading the book with them" (personal communication, December 9, 2020).

Arranging this type of preparatory communication with your guest speaker also lets them know what your class is particularly interested in learning. It shows them what your class already knows. It shows them you've already covered the basics (if you have) or alerts them to start from the beginning (if you haven't). It gives them the chance to be prepared to answer questions they may not normally field, and it also gives them advanced notice about any questions that they may not be willing or able to answer. This simple advanced preparation step is a win-win!

Questioning During Multi-Point Conferences

In these multi-point webinars, knowing that only a few questions will be answered, we recommend a different method of organizing your questions. Making a list of all questions your class has generated on a Word document (again, projected for all to see) or an interactive Padlet would be best for one very important reason: as the program progresses, it may be necessary to adjust which questions you're going to pose. When you only have two or three chances to ask a question of your expert, and all of a sudden some student down in Florida asks the exact same question that one of your pupils was going to, you need to be able to adjust and ask a different one on the fly.

My (Grayson's) class was participating in a webinar around Thanksgiving with some paleo-ornithologists who were explaining how dinosaurs were, in fact, related to modern birds. Perfect topic around turkey day, no? We were just about to ask how *T. rex* evolved into the turkey although most dinosaurs were wiped out by the Cretaceous–Paleogene (K–Pg) extinction event when another school in the multi-point conversation asked a very similar question. While we were disappointed that we didn't get to ask our version of the query, we were prepared with a list of quality replacements. Being prepared with a prioritized list of wonderings saved the day.

If you stick with your original question, not only does it waste the time of the expert, repeating something that has already been said, but it also wastes the time of all the participating schools. It can also suggest that your students were not listening carefully enough to realize the question had already been answered. As we learned when Skyping with Harvard graduate and award-winning writer Natasha Alford (@NatashaSAlford), a journalist should always have more questions prepared than there is time to answer them. When you do your homework and come prepared for an interview, you will leave with what you need to write your story. The same goes for learning from experts.

Low-Tech Is Okay

If technology just isn't your thing, questions written on notecards can do the trick in a pinch. This also can have some not-so-obvious advantages as well. One time while we were talking with a journalist via Zoom, our computer's microphone was just not cooperating. On their end, all they could hear was static. Fortunately for us, we had prepared our questions the old-fashioned way and had them written out on notecards. We were able to hold up the hand-written notes directly in front of the camera so that the newspaper reporter could see them. Low-tech saved the day, and he was able to answer our wonderings about journalism.

Ordering and Grouping Questions

By having questions pre-written and pre-approved, you can also shape the experience by ordering the questions in a way that would help to scaffold the conversation and make the dialogue flow smoothly. We recommend doing this with students beforehand so that you can talk through your own thinking. Do we group similar questions together, do we save the most hard-hitting questions for the end, so the tone of the conversation isn't confrontational? When you have multiple students asking similar questions, you could combine the questions into one with multiple parts, and have two or three students come up at once to split the question up evenly. This can also be a wonderful way for students who are differently-abled, English Learners, or just plain shy to gain confidence by speaking with a buddy. For example, we asked the following in a conversation with Airlie Anderson (@AirlieAnderson), author of the picture book *Neither:*

Student Script

CALEB: Hi, I'm Caleb.

QUIN: And I'm Quin.

CALEB: Of all the creative creature combinations you created for your book, why was the main motif one of chicks and bunnies?

QUIN: And what coffee shop were you in when you were inspired to draw such "interesting" creatures like eyeballs and bumble kittens for this book?

AIRLIE ANDERSON: Answers the questions...

BOTH: Thank you!

The Importance of Going "Off Script"

Of course, you can't plan out a script for the entire discussion. How boring would that be? Remember the scene from Monty Python's *The Meaning of Life*? "Good evening! Would you care for something to talk about?" the waiter asks as he hands the tongue-tied couple a set of conversation cue cards. If you were to have your students write out every single question ahead of time, leaving no room for spontaneity, you'd be making a colossal mistake.

First of all, by planning out each question in advance, you're assuming that you know everything you want to learn and that you know what they're going to say, but how could you? The most valuable piece of information that you can get from an interview with an expert is that which is an unexpected surprise! By giving your students a list of questions that they are devoted to, you close off all kinds of doors of opportunity before you've even started. As important as it is to help students become the developers of generative and meaningful questions, it is also equally important to teach them to remain open to new possibilities during the expert experience and adapt on the fly to fit the situation. To summarize, start with a plan but go with the flow!

START WITH A PLAN BUT GO WITH THE FLOW!
#ExpertEffectEDU

The most important thing to remember during the expert experience is that students should be aware of how to be an active listener. It shows respect for your guest expert and also helps you maximize your learning from the experience. You might feel like you're being an active listener on the inside, but it also needs to show on the outside. Here's what being an active listener looks like, sounds like, and feels like on this inside:

Expert Tips for Active Listening

Active Listening Looks Like...
- ❖ Paying Attention
  - ➤ Your eyes should be on the speaker. Don't miss out on what's being shown and shared!
- ❖ Assuming the Position
  - ➤ Your body needs to be in your optimal position for learning. Don't lay down, slouch, or get up and walk away during the lesson. This shows respect for the presenter.

Active Listening Sounds Like...
- ❖ Summarizing the Information
  - ➤ Repeat out loud and to the expert what you hear to make sure you've got it right.
- ❖ Asking Clarifying Questions
  - ➤ If something is confusing, ask a follow-up question to gain understanding.
- ❖ Sharing with a Friend Something that You Heard
  - ➤ What surprised you about what our expert said?
- ❖ One Person Speaking at a Time
  - ➤ Unless told otherwise, only one person's voice should be heard at once. Nobody wants to miss out on what's being said.

Active Listening Feels Like...
- ❖ Being Open-Minded
  - ➤ It's important to keep an open mind during new learning experiences. Try to understand where the other person is coming from and where the differences in opinion come from if they exist.
- ❖ Withholding Judgement
  - ➤ If the expert has said something that you find objectionable, wait until the appropriate time to voice your concern. Be patient. It may be later in the presentation, or after the lesson during your time to debrief.
- ❖ Reflecting on What's Being Said
  - ➤ Ask yourself some questions to help solidify the experience in your memory:
    - ■ Does this sound like something I've heard before?
    - ■ Does this sound like completely new information?
    - ■ How does this fit with what I knew or thought before?

Between advanced preparations with questions and being an active listener, your students will get a lot out of these opportunities. Like anything, the more chances you give them to practice talking and listening to experts, the more comfortable and proficient communicators they will become. This has come to pass for our classes year after year. You can see the experience pay off when joining multi-point conversations and watching other classes from around the country. As we look at their camera feeds, we see kids moving all around the classroom, making silly faces and dabbing when they see themselves on camera...and when we hear their questions, even those of older students, our elementary students always look at us and shake their heads. They are sometimes shocked by the immaturity and the unprofessionalism of other students who have not done the homework to prepare for taking full advantage of these experiences.

One time we were Skyping with a group of scientists in Colorado who had just completed a series of computerized tomography (CT) scans on the two mummies they housed at their museum with the help of a local children's hospital. When the turn of questioning went to a high school group in New York, they asked, "Are the mummies wrapped in toilet paper?" One fifth-grader turned to me and disapprovingly said, "I guess they didn't do their research." When students are regularly given a chance to speak with experts, they see themselves as colleagues or peers with the experts who are on the same journey of discovery. This is the kind of maturity and confidence in speaking with professionals we want our learners to gain.

Ending the Experience

If we can leave you with one more tip as well, it would be to always leave the conversation open-ended at the close. We always like to ask a question that goes something like this, "Thank you so much for your time and expertise today. Is there anything else that you often get asked that we've left out, or is there anything else you'd like to tell us?" After listening to this answer, we always like to give students one more chance to think about themselves stepping into the shoes of the guest. We ask them if there is any advice they'd like to give students who are thinking about pursuing a career path similar to their own. It's never too early for children to start thinking about what they want to be when they grow up...even if their dreams or that job evolves by the time they get there.

After the Expert Experience

Video calls with experts from afar are great starting points to initiate a deeper discussion with your students about whatever the topic is at hand. Below, you'll find some questions you can use to further discuss and analyze what you have learned from the call with the expert.

Debrief Questions

- What are the key lessons/ideas/information we have learned?
- How can you use what you have learned?
- What did you notice or think was most interesting about the interview?
- Why did you notice that/think that?
- Why is this important?
- Does that happen in your life or school? Why?
- How can we use that information?
- What new questions do you now have?

Thank-Yous

It's always nice to have students write a thank you note to the guest teacher after the experience is through. The best types of thank yous can also serve the dual purpose of acting as an exit slip that allows you a glimpse into their thinking. A super-easy writing prompt that students can include in their thank you is an "I Used to Think...But Now I Think" routine. In this way, students can not only reflect on how their thinking about the topic has changed, but it also allows the expert to see the impact they have had on your class! This is an extremely gratifying gesture for the experts, as it shows them that their time spent was worthwhile. If the outside expert is a part of your local community or a family member to one of your students, hand-written notes delivered through the mail or sent home in a backpack would be completely appropriate.

If, however, your expert comes from further abroad, there are still more creative ways to say thanks.

One time, while co-teaching, our school hosted a visiting author, Mark Newman. Newman is the author of *Super Yooper,* a series of children's books that chronicle the work of environmental superhero Billy Cooper, who defends the Great Lakes from invasive species such as the rusty crayfish and sea lampreys from his headquarters in the Upper Peninsula of Michigan, where residents are lovingly known as "Yoopers" (U.P.-ers). Newman visits schools across the region, sharing about how he and his creative partner got their start creating public service billboards that addressed issues such as racism, environmental health, and AIDS. The students, inspired by this effective activism, wanted to try their own hands at it.

Zach and I passed out large index cards and told them to make a mini version of a billboard they would like to see in our area that combined the same aspects of Newman's own creative themes of humor, social responsibility, and environmentalism. As our young activists finished their billboard prototypes, they recorded a video message explaining their creative thought process and how it tied into what they had learned from the visiting expert. When they were done, we collected their responses on Flipgrid and sent the author the link to our grid. In this way, he was able to hear the children's ideas, see the impact his visit had had on them, and could even respond with short video messages of his own. In our opinion, this is a transformational application of technology...to the modification or redefinition order of the SAMR model (more on this in Chapter 13)...sending thank you notes in a 21st-century modality that focuses on the process of the project and the learning of the experience.

10 TOOLS OF THE TRADE

> *It's not the tool, but the user of the tool that makes the difference.*
>
> –JENNIFER CASA-TODD (@JCASATODD)

The iPhone is officially older than every single one of our fourth- and fifth-grade students. Let that sink in for a moment. Apple released its initial version of FaceTime in 2010. Every child in our classroom knows how to video call their grandparents. (Maybe more impressive, most grandparents know how to FaceTime them back!) With this type of technology at our fingertips for over a decade, it's past time that we start including it into our teaching on a regular basis.

We're here to provide you with ideas for incorporating distance learning opportunities with free programs like Zoom, Skype, and Google Hangouts. In this way, students receive first-hand experience across content areas, tapping into the knowledge and expertise of experts in the field. Using this equipment for virtual field trips can help improve observation and perception skills, and offer students global connections in an innovative model that would not be possible in a stand-alone classroom. We are very proud to say that our students learn in the classroom with the world at their fingertips, and now you will be able to say that too!

Zoom

Zoom seemed to come along and take a huge "come-from-behind" type victory over Skype when the whole world shut down due to COVID-19 and school, meetings, happy hours, birthday parties, and game nights went virtual. This seems to be the go-to video conferencing app for these experiences going forward—especially if school districts are purchasing the full version for teachers in preparation for a possibility of more remote learning to come. One thing we love about Zoom is that you send a link to the other person as opposed to them having to answer a call or add them as a contact like you do on Skype. Other awesome features include breakout rooms, participant reactions, audience polls, built-in chat, and Q & A features for webinars with experts.

Skype

If we had published this book in 2019, the only platform you would have heard us mention would have been Skype. Microsoft's video conferencing platform was the OG (original go-to) of connecting classrooms with experts. Part of the reason for Skype's success was its ease of use, functioning much like an old-fashioned telephone call with some bonus features. The other part of it was because Microsoft had spent many years developing "Skype in the Classroom" on education.skype.com, which at one time held a huge database where you could find live Skype events, virtual field trips, guest speakers, and even collaborative projects your students could work on alongside others from around the world. Unfortunately, their site has been decommissioned as of December 2020. Skype could still be useful to classrooms if your district utilizes the rest of the 365 products, apps, and services. But frankly, even Microsoft seems to have moved on from Skype in exchange for Teams, which offers many impressive video conferencing features. Users can host 1080p calls with up to 250 members, with the included ability to share screens and record calls in a manner very similar to Zoom.

FaceTime

During a recent conference that was attended by several educators from our district, we had the luxury of getting an hour and a half for our lunch break. We felt like we had died and gone to heaven since the norm for us typically involves taking a 30-second bathroom-break, scarfing down our food, *maybe* sneaking a second K-cup from the Keurig machine, and racing back to class to prepare for the afternoon of learning. During this windfall, we had gotten the chance to share our ideas for this book with an administrator in our district.

We were so excited to tell him about all of the ways in which we had been getting our students to learn from experts and make their learning real…when he quickly cut in to remind us of a very important fact. He said that in his opinion, the number one source of expertise comes from within our existing school communities. Using people who are close to your students, such as other teachers they've known, family members, and trusted neighbors, helps to make the learning more relevant and meaningful for students. If these members are not available to come into the classroom to chat for any reason, FaceTime is a great way to connect.

FaceTime is a lot more intimate than Skype by the mere fact that it involves connecting with someone who is already in your phone's list of contacts. It means sharing a personal phone number, and for some reason, this feels more intimate than sharing a Skype username or a Zoom link. (Perhaps because it includes the risk that you may accidentally butt-dial them at a later date.) The only downside to FaceTime is that at the time of writing this, only eight users are capable of connecting at once. Furthermore, screen sharing is not supported.

For people you know personally, or for those in your own school community, FaceTime may be the best choice. For one thing, if you have an Apple device, it requires no additional installation of extraneous apps or setting up of separate accounts. This can be especially nice if the expert on the other end doesn't communicate with school children regularly, and therefore may be unfamiliar with other commonly used apps. Your student's mom, who may be an engineer at Tesla, might not have a

Skype account set up, but could carry an iPhone (unless she's one of those green-bubble-texter-types).

One of the teachers we work with was recently studying the community in which we live as a part of a social studies unit and was aware that our former principal now worked as a volunteer firefighter at the local fire station. Unable to bring her class on an impromptu field trip to visit the firehouse, she was able to call him up using FaceTime, which allowed him to take her class on a virtual tour of the station by carrying his phone around. They were able to see all the same sights, ask the same questions, and learn the same facts as if they had gone in person, but the FaceTime call with a familiar former member of our school community made it possible to accomplish the same goals!

We'll share one more story to illustrate how FaceTime can build a great bridge between your school and community. To celebrate *March is Reading Month*, teachers always invite "mystery readers" to come in and read a story to the class. We make a Sign-Up Genius so that parents, grandparents, or other family members can sign up to come read. We feel very fortunate to teach in an extremely diverse school district, which often means grandparents live on different continents. Thanks to Face-Time, we have not only had guest readers at our school who live in the surrounding neighborhood, but also from India, Pakistan, Sri Lanka, and many other countries who could read a story to the class through the camera on their phone. Also, with the current nature of our learning environment due to the COVID-19 Pandemic, it feels like actual guest readers coming into our classrooms are a thing of the past (we hope they aren't), but we can utilize this technology to continue having guest readers throughout March and beyond.

Google Suite

Google remains king in our minds for all things collaborative. Whether it be a shared document, slide presentation, or survey form for feedback, Google is our go-to. They also have their own video chatting and communication apps, in the form of Google Chat, Rooms, and Meet. These are easy to get started with if you have G Suite through your school district. These tools allow you to talk face to face from your computer or mobile device, make free video calls with up to 150 people, and perhaps most impressively, start a video call or chat right in Gmail or your Google calendar by instantly going from an email conversation or calendar event to a group video call or project workroom.

I (Grayson) used Google Hangouts (now known as Meet) for perhaps one of the coolest virtual field trips of all time, when our class got to watch a deployment of the deep-diving manned submarine, Alvin, from on deck of a ship in the middle of the Pacific Ocean. Yes, the same Alvin that was involved in the discovery and exploration of the wreck of the HMS Titanic. It was remarkable to get to talk to the actual scientists involved in the exploration of hydrothermal vents at the bottom of the seafloor and watch as they lowered the rover into the water for another dive...live!

Other Video Conferencing Applications

Some of the above-mentioned applications are especially useful to virtual learning providers who want to be able to connect to multiple schools at the same time. Unlike FaceTime, Zoom and Google allow more than a handful of users to be connected at once, and there is also the option to switch between the multiple video feeds and share user screens. You may, however, find that some virtual program providers will opt to use different applications entirely, such as Facebook Live, YouTube Live, Cisco Webex, BlueJeans, Remo, GoBrunch, or others—different companies that all do similar tasks. Thanks to the COVID-19 pandemic, tech companies around the world have been tripping over themselves to fill the need for reliable video conferencing software, and teachers and their students have been the direct beneficiaries of their hard work! The only tip we can give you is to check with your provider to see what platform they use and do a test run to make sure everything is working before the connection is made.

Hardware Requirements

At the risk of sounding very "inexpert," we want to share a quick and embarrassing story about the early years of connecting our students to experts. When we co-taught, the only technology we had at our disposal were iPads, an Apple TV, and a projector. In the early days of Skyping with experts, we would call them using Skype on the iPad, then AirPlay to the Apple TV, and project this to the SMART Board. It mostly worked. Sometimes, the sound would not work or would be lagging behind the video, and at other times, the video would freeze, and we'd only have sound. Once, we even had to disconnect the AirPlay and had to finish the call from the iPad itself. Imagine the fifty-six 4th-graders trying to huddle in around the 10-inch screen, listening intently to the output from the tiny speakers. We know that technology issues can be frustrating, but the benefits can be great once you get the hang of it. We have since sought to make things simpler for us and for the other teachers we work with and would like to share some pointers with you.

To make connecting with experts around the world easy for the teachers in our own school building, we assembled two mobile video conferencing carts which we lovingly call "The World on Wheels." Through the process of successfully writing multiple grants, we gathered webcams, large flat-screen TVs, TV carts, laptop computers, and high-quality microphones. We wanted to make the experience as easy as possible for all students in our school to have access to learning from experts from afar. In this way, we were giving teachers the ability to check out the cart, roll it into their classroom, plug it in for the expert experience, and when they were finished, they could just roll it away. You don't need to write grants to accomplish this, though. You can have a successful connection with minimal technology. Think about these five key areas when planning future connections:

Internet Connection

Most schools should be good with this, having the infrastructure to support either wired or wireless devices. Desktops, laptops, tablets, and even phones are all going to get the job done. Make sure your wireless connection is going to be strong enough to support video conferencing, and if it's not, maybe consider plugging in your device to an ethernet port, or moving your class to another place in your school where the signal is stronger, such as a library or multi-purpose room.

Sound Capture

Most devices have built-in microphones nowadays, but if your desktop is like mine—old, possibly haunted, spiteful, and decrepit—you may not be ready to connect just yet. Stand-alone microphones that connect via Bluetooth, USB, or audio jack cables will make it possible for your students to be heard.

Sound Output

Built-in speakers may not be powerful enough to allow all students to easily hear what's being said from around the room. Does your computer have an external audio option? The setup we normally default to is connecting the laptop, making the connection to the TV via an HDMI cable, which then sends the sound directly through the TV's speakers for a much fuller sound. Alternatively, you could bring a set of extra computer speakers from home or connect your laptop to a Bluetooth speaker to boost your volume for the whole group to hear.

Video Capture

If you're using a mobile device or laptop, chances are there will be a built-in camera, but if you're using a desktop, you may need to spring for an external webcam. These are not very expensive at all, and often they will give you added features like an external microphone and a fisheye lens that will make it easier for your expert to hear you clearly and see your whole class at once.

Video Output

As we shared in the story of how we got our start, getting your whole class to gather around a small screen is not fun, so consider how you'll be allowing everyone to see what's going on. Connecting your computer to a projector would be the go-to, or if you have an extra flatscreen TV lying around, you could go so far as to build your own "World on Wheels" mobile cart to get your whole school in on the action.

Part I: Think + Tweet
#ExpertEffectEDU

1. How can we keep students engaged throughout their learning career?
2. How do we create learning opportunities that focus on empowerment instead of compliance?
3. Think of some specific areas of your curriculum. To what outside experts can you connect your students to deepen their learning?
4. Shout out and name drop! To whom have you connected your class, and how did the experience benefit your learners? We want to hear about the experts out there who are willing and able to help our kids!
5. How does seeking out a wide variety of guest experts diversify the educational narrative for your students?
6. To what places might you take a virtual field trip to help students understand more? Look it up or reach out; it could be easier to arrange than you think!
7. What far-out places or interesting experiences are in your curriculum that you could have students "experience" using virtual reality?
8. What field trips close to school could you take to enhance learning for your students?
9. Dream big! If it were possible to go anywhere, where would you want your class to visit? A dream field trip is a destination that might be a long shot, but it should still be possible. Don't let the sticker price of these ventures scare you off! Grants, academic gains, and students' families' desire to support you can all influence your ability to go and make the cost of the trip more manageable.

PART II
STUDENTS BECOME THE EXPERTS

11 PROJECT-BASED LEARNING

STUDENTS NEED THE CHANCE TO PLAY THE ROLE OF THE PROFESSIONAL, WORKING ON AN AUTHENTIC TASK THAT COULD BE TAKEN ON BY THE TRUE EXPERT.
#ExpertEffectEDU

We think, as with so many other things in life, that when you're on the outside of a subject, it's easier to say, "No thanks, learning about that is not really my cup of tea." But when you get hands-on and closer to the circle of people living in the field and producing content in the area, it becomes a totally different story.

That's what becoming your own expert means to us: becoming so immersed in the topic, having learned from experts outside of the classroom, that you yourself are now ready to also produce something of value to those outside your own learning environment, thereby fulfilling one of the aims of our classroom mission statement: to advance and improve the lives of others.

The purpose of this section of our book is not to explain all the elements of Project-Based Learning. Simply put, we are not the "experts" on PBL (see what we did there?). There are so many people and organizations who are more qualified than us to explain the entire PBL process. (We highly recommend you check out pblworks.org and their many resources.) Our purpose of including this in our book is to show how Project-based Learning has transformed our classroom culture, how it puts the responsibility on the students to become "experts" of their learning, and later, how it becomes their responsibility to make their learning process public to an authentic audience.

In the summer of 2018, I (Zach) attended a two-day Project-based Learning workshop that changed the way I viewed teaching and learning. The training was led by Myla Lee (@MyTLee2) of PBLWorks (formerly known as the Buck Institute for Education). She and her organization are the true leaders and pioneers of Project-Based Learning. Learning about the "Gold-Standard of PBL" model gave me a crystal clear picture as to what PBL was and the potential it could have in my classroom. As originally written in *Setting the Standard for Project-Based Learning*, authors John Larmer, John Mergendoller, and Suzie Boss share the Gold Standard for PBL with seven essential elements. Check out the following link to familiarize yourself.

https://www.pblworks.org/what-is-pbl/gold-standard-project-design

The ironic thing about this training is that going into it, I would have told you I was already doing Project-based Learning in my classroom. In the past, I had dabbled with projects and had already seen the engagement in my classroom increase. About an hour into the training though, I was struck with the realization that I had only been doing *elements* of true Project-based Learning. What I had been doing was *PBL-ish*. I had viewed PBL as a reward for students to partake in at the end of the unit, instead of a vehicle for their learning throughout the unit. I was having students do projects only at the very end of a unit as a capstone to their learning. They weren't quite "cookie-cutter projects"—they had a choice in how they presented their information, but still, it was a culmination and an extension, not an essential part of the learning process from the start.

It might as well have been called the "tombstone" rather than the "capstone" because all of the learning died at the end—graded, buried, and forgotten. Trevor Muir calls these kinds of last-minute add-ons "dessert projects"—not necessary to the actual learning and sometimes better if left on the plate. "The dessert is just an add-on," he says, "a follow-up to the meal" (Muir, 2018). Project-Based Learning shouldn't be something to only come at the end of a unit—it should be the main course. In order for students to truly learn through the process of the project, we believe that students need the chance to play the role of the professional, working on an authentic task that could be taken on by the true expert *throughout* their unit of study.

The most important part of effective Project-Based Learning is for students to start with a captivating driving question. This question needs to be asked at the onset of learning. It is the touchstone to which you return after every lesson, using it to check in on your progress along the way. And honestly, developing one is probably the hardest part of the process.

At first, students come up with very surface-level questions that can be answered with a simple Google search. We need students to come up with questions that don't have a simple answer, which students have to dig at. One rule of thumb that we like to go by is that a question that could be answered by a single word or phrase is probably not a deep, guiding question. For example, you wouldn't want to ask a presidential historian at Monticello when Thomas Jefferson was born. You wouldn't want to ask a world-famous author with whom you have limited time to speak when her birthday is. It wouldn't help you understand her writing process, her thoughts behind character decisions, or to get advice on the writing process! We've both experienced that as you engage your students in more opportunities for Project-Based Learning, coming up with a driving question becomes easier and more natural.

Another important aspect of the PBL process is that we, as teachers, get excited about the learning as well. We will both freely admit that we don't always jump out of bed in the morning fired up to teach the numerous causes of the American Revolution, the various methods of long division, or...really...anything to do with fractions. But when our classes are engaged in a meaningful and purposeful project, we are excited to help them with their learning and their creations. Your energy as an educator is contagious. If you are excited about a project, we know your students will be too.

Let's compare two examples: one from my first year of teaching and one from this past year to show how my thinking has evolved to create more opportunities for Project-Based Learning.

Example One: While studying how Michigan became a state, students read a chapter in the textbook while the teacher reads aloud. The class discusses how Michigan essentially traded the city of Toledo to Ohio for the western 80% of the Upper Peninsula. Students can't believe the trade. Four days later, after a few more lessons and a review, students take a multiple-choice test that is provided along with the prescribed curriculum.

Example Two: Students and teachers read together and discuss the Toledo War and how the conflict was solved by trading the Upper Peninsula for Toledo. Students begin to inquire why Ohio would want to give that much land to Michigan and why Michigan wanted Toledo. Instead of answering the questions, these become the driving questions for this mini-project. Students can choose which side to be on—Michigan or Ohio—and the teacher lets students know that in three days, they will be having a Michigan vs. Ohio debate. They will present their evidence as to why they want each side to win. (This also works quite well around the big rivalry week of University of Michigan vs. Ohio State in college football.) The debate rages on, as students know they must have their evidence in line and be prepared to respond to rebuttals.

In which of these two examples do you think students would remember the content and be more engaged in the learning process?

When students are engaged in a project, they are allowed to be creative, solve problems, and come up with solutions. Learning feels like a discovery, not something that is simply told to them by a teacher standing in front of the room. This is the kind of meaningful learning that gets remembered—learning which sparks excitement that teachers and students alike will use to energize them throughout the year.

LEARNING SHOULD FEEL LIKE DISCOVERING SOMETHING NEW, NOT SIMPLY BEING TOLD A FACT.
#ExpertEffectEDU

In this example, students engaged in a three-day mini-project. It did not take weeks, months, or the whole year, but it was enough to truly engage students in the learning process of researching and finding out why this seemingly lopsided trade went through. From our experience in working with teachers, it seems that people can get intimidated by the idea that their projects have to be these huge undertakings that take months, but that needn't be the case. Some of the most powerful learning experiences in our classrooms take place in these short-term mini-projects.

12 THREE ESSENTIAL INGREDIENTS FOR PBL

> *The single problem plaguing all students in all schools everywhere is the crisis of disconnection.*

–ADAM FLETCHER (@BICYCLINGFISH)

A s teachers, we're often prompted to think back to our educational experiences during sessions of professional development and Twitter chats. It always fascinates us how little we actually remember from being in elementary school. In a way, it kind of takes the pressure off of us to know that our students will certainly not remember the many mistakes we make throughout the day or year. But we find there's even more power in analyzing the things we actually do remember even years later.

Right now, we challenge you to take a moment to think about the learning experiences that stick out to you—the ones you still remember today. What are your favorite learning memories? What did you do in school that you still remember today? For me (Zach), it was my third-grade project studying the state of Connecticut. This was important to me because I had family members who lived there, so I had visited. I could call and ask them questions; it was personal to me.

Another project that I clearly remember, and probably the most powerful learning experience of my whole educational experience, is the time in fourth grade when I got to create and record a radio show with my friend Mark. I was never a kid who loved homework or even much of my school work, but during this project, I was completely engaged. We spent hours at my house with my dad helping us to record and rerecord (on a cassette tape) until our broadcast was absolutely perfect. We were laughing, learning, and fully enjoying the process. I still have that cassette tape to this day. (The only problem is that I have no way to play it!)

What's the common thread between these learning opportunities? They were projects. I created something. I owned my learning. I had a choice in the process. When we stop to reflect and distill the magic of these memories into a recreatable formula, the three commonalities with these types of projects are the three essential ingredients in the Project-Based learning recipe: voice, choice, and creativity. And thinking about it now, we've really been advocates for Project-Based Learning since childhood.

Search the handbook of any educational technology conference; we can assure you that you will find many sessions based on the promise of increasing student engagement. At an earlier stage of our careers, we might have pointed you to a cool new app and said students were more excited about learning because of it. And while that might have been the case, it was only surface-level engagement lasting for a short amount of time.

We have found that true engagement is more than just a cool app, though. It's really about asking better questions, expecting more from our students, and tapping into issues that students truly care about. As a teacher, our job is not as much solely delivering content, but framing our content in ways that gets our students amped up to learn about it. Our job is to dip our content in kerosene and find the spark that sets the process on fire (metaphorically speaking, of course).

TRUE ENGAGEMENT IS MORE THAN JUST A COOL APP. IT'S REALLY ABOUT ASKING BETTER QUESTIONS, EXPECTING MORE FROM STUDENTS, AND TAPPING INTO ISSUES THAT STUDENTS TRULY CARE ABOUT.
#ExpertEffectEDU

When we do this effectively, we see students on fire with a passion for learning about topics they normally wouldn't care about. As one of my (Grayson's) students said on a stage in front of 1,000 educators on our district's opening day keynote in 2019,

> *We didn't just learn about social studies through reading a history textbook, we relived the past through Project-based Learning. If I would have only read about Joliet and Marquette, I probably would have forgotten about them within a day. But, I became them, people! I built the boat that they took on their journey of discovery. Yes, it was made out of cardboard, but I built it!*
>
> *–ERIC, CLASS OF 2026*

There are so many little gems of wisdom in this student quote, but mainly, when we let students have agency over their learning, the engagement comes naturally. Imagine a world in which the roles of students and teachers are realigned...students no longer passive recipients of information, but instead partners in learning through the educational process. It's through this fundamental realignment and the following three ingredients that we believe the crisis of student disengagement can be solved.

Ingredient #1: Voice

We have found over and over again that when we create Project-based Learning experiences that allow students to amplify their own voice, it raises the bar and gets kids excited about learning. We are not saying that every learning activity has to be like this...we still give math tests and worksheets after all...but our goal is to create enough of these big experiences throughout the year that students will one day write about *us* in a book 20+ years later (just kidding, but that would be pretty cool)!

As I mentioned, in fourth grade, my friend and I got to be the producers, editors, and voice talent behind our very own radio show. I am positive that, in some way, this experience as a student is the reason my class would one day go on to start the *4th-Grade Innovators Podcast*...a launchpad from which we can recreate some of those same feelings of ownership and accomplishment in our present-day classroom.

It's important to note that no two classrooms employing the process of PBL will (or should) look the same. There are infinite iterations and combinations of students and teachers, each with their own skills and passions. Our own classes' projects don't even look the same from year to year because we have completely new groups of students each time September rolls around! In fact, if two classrooms "doing" PBL were to look the same, I would throw down a penalty flag and stop the game! If you're using something you found on Teachers Pay Teachers and it looks exactly like your neighbor's across the hallway, something's definitely not working right, and the message of Project-Based Learning has been lost in translation.

To us, giving students a chance to use their voice and feed their passion also means that it's okay for different students to approach the same project from different angles. In the same way that no two students will have identical viewpoints, beliefs, or opinions, no two projects will end up looking the same. When students are tapping into their own unique passions and learning about something personally meaningful to them, their unique and special voice is what comes through loud and clear.

Ingredient #2: Choice

In my third-grade geography project, I got to choose to study the state of Connecticut. Had I been assigned another state with no connection to me, I would not have enjoyed or remembered this process, and I surely wouldn't be writing about it in a book twenty-one years later. No one likes to be told what to do all day long. People like to have a choice over what or how they will do things. Having choices makes people feel in control. When we give students choices, we allow them to feel in control of their learning.

In the book, *The Highly Engaged Classroom*, Dr. Robert Marzano explains, "Research has shown that providing choices to students of all age levels often increases their intrinsic motivation. Choice in the classroom has also been linked to increases in student effort, task performance, and subsequent learning" (Marzano, 2013, p. 14).

Now please don't think we need to go to the extreme with this and say, "You can do the math workbook today or can play Fortnite. The choice is yours!" We all know what would happen if we did that. But even giving students small choices throughout the day makes them feel more in control. There's one key to making sure student choice is effectively used in the classroom, a magic formula, if you will. We're going to whisper this, so the students don't hear this classified information... ready? *The key to giving students choices in the classroom is to make sure that you, as their teacher, are happy with whatever choice they make.* Mind-blowing right?

One way to do this is to allow students to demonstrate their learning in a way that works for them. Example: "Explain the events leading up to the American Revolution. You can write it out on paper, create a Keynote Presentation, make a poster or even a video explaining it." No matter what they choose, we will be able to see if they understand the concept or not.

Giving students the freedom to choose certain aspects of their learning may seem scary. We get it. It feels as though you're giving away a bit of your control over the classroom. It may look a little chaotic to the untrained eye. But the amazing thing about freedom is the more you give away, the more you truly have. Giving students choice is like making that biweekly investment into your 403(b) retirement plan. It feels sad and scary to see money coming out of your paycheck, but in the long run, it will pay out dividends. When students are given a chance to use their voice and choose how their learning looks, they will be more "invested" in school (see what we did there?).

When It Comes to Student Choice, What Stays the Same For All?

Same Driving Question: When students are given choices, all of their options will still fall under the same big umbrella that is your class's driving question. Usually, the driving question comes from witnessing some initial phenomena or event. For example, if studying the effects of pollution on the Earth's ocean habitats, the whole class may watch a short YouTube video about "Plastic Island," the great Pacific Garbage Patch. As a class, you then start to wonder, "What caused this mess, and how are people working to fix this gigantic problem?" In finding out more, there are a million and one ways to differentiate, but the same basic question should bind the class together on a common quest.

Same Learning Outcomes: In the end, you eventually want students to know basically the same information. The nice thing is that while one group may be researching the effects of pollution on whales, and another group is researching oceanic clean-up technology, they will eventually both know the same things once the groups have gotten a chance to present their findings to their peers (more on teaching others as experts in Part III).

Same Time Frame: While some groups may finish earlier and other groups might take longer, you can feel okay requiring students to complete their learning in about the same amount of time, give or take a few days. The nice thing is when you are allowing groups who finished early to present to the class, the other groups who need more time are given those presentation days to wrap things up. Be flexible with your deadlines—it's better to allow students the time they need to create something they're proud of rather than rushing them to turn in junk.

Same Learning Standards: The nice thing about standards is that they are purposefully written very broadly. We'll give you one example.

English Language Arts Standards; Language; Grade 5: "Use knowledge of language and its conventions when writing, speaking, reading, or listening" (Common Core State Standards, 2009). How vague is that? Thankfully, no matter what topic the students are researching and presenting on, every student will be given the opportunity to expand, combine, and reduce sentences for meaning, reader/listener interest, and style.

When It Comes to Student Choice, How Can You Differentiate?

Different Interests and Related Subtopics: This is where the choices really begin to be visible. While the entire class is still learning about the same main topic, differentiating the subtopics to suit student interest is where you get the passion and excitement in student learning. While my (Grayson's) class was once learning about Native American cultures in North America, I had a very...active...group of boys. They would not have typically been described as enthusiastic about school. During this unit, however, I suggested they become experts about all the various types of tools and weapons used by various Indigenous groups. What they ended up learning and creating astounded me. They researched, built replicas, wrote an entire script, and eventually staged a play for our class in the style of a show that was popular at the time, Deadliest Warrior. They explained the various tools used by different groups and taught about an aspect of the topic in which they were especially interested. Without giving them the freedom to explore an aspect that they cared about, and without the choice to create an engaging skit, it may have been like herding cats to get them to do much of anything.

Different Types of Learning Materials: One size definitely does not fit all when it comes to learning materials. While it's important to help students to develop their ability to glean information from traditional non-fiction texts, such as your textbook, there are now more resources at our disposal than ever before, and these volumes of knowledge will only continue to grow exponentially. BrainPOP videos, FreedomFlix, actual real-life experts, Newsela articles, Discovery Education, YouTube, Hoopla, Epic!, Wonderopolis...the list goes on. Don't try and force the square peg into the round hole—allow students to explore resources that are accessible and exciting for them in their quest to become the expert.

Different End Products: This is the part of the project cycle that students get most excited about. We require students to share their learning, but *how* they share their learning is left up to them. We have seen amazing final products come from both high tech and low tech. Some possibilities are that students can create a website, a video, a slideshow presentation, a blog, record a podcast episode, they can write a script and do a live reenactment, or build a model. The possibilities are endless as long as they can showcase what they learned and answer the driving question. This also helps make presentation day much more enjoyable than watching eight of the exact same slideshow presentations back-to-back-to-back.

Different Authentic Audiences: While you, the teacher, will almost always be a main part of the audience, watching and listening to what your students have learned, there is a lot to be gained from creating varied audiences for your students—inviting other classes in, sending links to blogs to family members, sharing videos with buddy classes from around the globe...the sky's the limit. (Much more on this in Part III.)

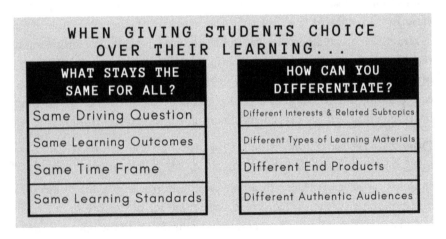

WHEN GIVING STUDENTS CHOICE OVER THEIR LEARNING...

WHAT STAYS THE SAME FOR ALL?	HOW CAN YOU DIFFERENTIATE?
Same Driving Question	Different Interests & Related Subtopics
Same Learning Outcomes	Different Types of Learning Materials
Same Time Frame	Different End Products
Same Learning Standards	Different Authentic Audiences

Ingredient #3: Creativity

Now, we will try to convince you to go against the oldest sayings in the teacher's handbook, "There's no point in trying to reinvent the wheel." Have you heard this one uttered by a colleague before? It's usually said right before they tell the new teacher to keep their head down, don't make waves, don't get noticed, and don't rock the boat. We have no doubts that there have been plenty of teachers who have tried something new, only to be reprimanded by the administration for doing something outside the normal routine without running it by them first or being talked about in the teachers' lounge for "making us all look bad.". You yourself may have been burned while attempting something really cool for your students. I (Grayson) was once rejected in an interview for another administrative position because of my thinking. I was told, "There are just certain things that kids have to know, and sometimes you have to spoon-feed them in the way they've always known, and their parents have always known." No joke. But for those who live by the mantra, "We've always done it that way," let me try to convince you that reinventing the wheel can actually be a good thing for you AND your students.

The way in which I relate this mentality to education is this: there is no excuse for ever doing the same thing, in the same way, more than once. Even if it's a really cool thing, there are still always ways you can grow, make it newer…an improved iteration, making it better than before. I'd challenge you to never settle for something that was good enough for someone else or for when you did it the year before. Our blog's tagline is as follows:

WHEN IT COMES TO INNOVATION, THERE IS NO FINISH LINE.
#ExpertEffectEDU

We say this because you will never have the "perfect" year when you can throw down the microphone and say, "Seacrest out!" Even if things feel like they are going really well, there's always something that you can tweak to make it better. Don't settle for "good enough."

Here's a quick anecdote. During my first year of teaching, I (Grayson) was determined to stay organized. After each math lesson, I saved the transparency copy I had made to use on the overhead projector (yes, I'm that old) in a hanging folder in a giant filing cabinet next to my desk. In this way, I told myself, I would never have to reinvent the wheel or make these tedious copies ever again. I believed I was working smarter, not harder, by preparing myself for the following year.

This is a trap that too many teachers fall into. When I see copies left behind on the copy machine, with a trademarked date of 1999, or when teachers pay for and download a file from Teachers Pay Teachers to store away on their hard drive, it is evidence of a lack of innovation. The worst is when a letter gets sent home to parents, and the dates are still the same from the previous year! Again, I can joke about this because it's happened to me. It is safer, it is easier, and it is quicker to use existing content and reuse old copies, but in my opinion, it is by no means better for students.

So here is our challenge to you: before you print off thirty more copies of your "oldie but goodie" worksheets, think about it again through new eyes with your current students in mind. How can you change it to fit your students' needs better? How can you take it to the next level? Think of a way to make things interesting, new, and novel for your students this year and always. Our students deserve our best and most innovative approach, not a has-been reprint.

A simple rule of thumb is this: if it's not exciting for you, it won't be for your students. Your learners are not robots. They're human beings who follow the same rules of learning as everyone else. Learning happens when they are intrigued, perplexed, and curious...so mix it up and keep it fresh!

There was a tweet we came across last year made by a popular edu-influencer on Twitter that served as a wake-up call to me. As soon as I read it, I knew I had to do something right away to change things up. Children deserve to learn through fun, challenge, and authenticity. If I was going to do something boring, there was zero chance that the learning would "stick." I ditched the math lesson I had "planned" (read from the teacher's edition) and made up a new game on the spot. It didn't require much…just some dice and a recording sheet thrown together in Word, and I had a new way to get my students to practice what I wanted them to learn.

We would push for teachers, both new and experienced, to really learn their jobs by doing it, rather than finding what's out there and making copies of someone else's lessons. Constructing your lessons from scratch will yield the same result as making home-cooked meals with fresh ingredients, rather than buying prepackaged or pre-cooked meals that are ready-to-eat…more delicious and more nutritious. "But I'm a terrible 'cook," you say? Constructing lesson plans for your students is part of the job of being a professional teacher. We all need to continue to learn how to do this in the best way possible. We're not saying that every single lesson needs a complete makeover. Still, it's our job to evaluate the needs and interests of our students and to find opportunities to allow for deeper learning when the need arises. Trying to turn each history lesson into a simulation of the Continental Congress would induce teacher burn-out quickly. Pace yourself, add a little more vigor each year, and always remain open to those flashes of inspiration.

There's a great Adidas ad campaign that uses the hashtag #ORIGINALis. Think of yourself as an original. Never stop reinventing your classroom, your lessons, yourself as a teacher because neither learning nor lesson plans are one-size-fits-all. On our journey to push creativity forward, #ORIGINALis never finished.

NEITHER LEARNING NOR LESSON PLANS ARE ONE-SIZE-FITS-ALL.
#ExpertEffectEDU

Confession Time: Two Truths and a Lie

Truth 1: Not all Projects will be Perfect.

Often we look at "Edu-Twitter" or "Teacher-Gram" and see these incredible examples of Project-based Learning which immediately triggers the "my students could never do that" type of thinking and spurs unhealthy comparisons between ourselves and others. It's always important to remember that social media is a *highlight reel*, not necessarily a representation of every project.

We have both had students whose projects flopped. Something didn't work out. The tech failed. Their epic cardboard creation representing a historical event collapsed. Yes, we've even had tears.

But you know what? We can guarantee you those students still learned more than if they had read a textbook and taken a multiple-choice test. I've never seen students cry over a textbook passage, so even if the project didn't work out, it's clear the passion was still there. (Please note—tears are never our goal.) When students' passion gets involved in the project, we know we have done our job.

With Project-Based Learning, it's so much more about the process than the final project anyway. In this process of creation, true learning is taking place whether the final product turns out perfectly or not.

Truth 2: Project-Based Learning Takes Time!

Ask any teacher their biggest concern with just about anything in education, and you'll surely hear the word "time." We won't sugar coat it; PBL takes more time. But more importantly, we have witnessed that the time spent is well worth it.

Teachers live in a world of trying to stomach our lunch in fifteen minutes while making copies, a world in which some days we feel lucky if we have a chance to take a bathroom break. With all the new curriculum initiatives, we can fall into the trap of thinking we can't take ONE. MORE. THING.

In a memorable blog post titled "Making Time for Project-Based Learning," author John Spencer puts it better than we ever could by writing, "PBL isn't about adding something new to your plate. It's about rearranging your plate with a focus on student voice and choice" (Spencer, 2018). It's a common misconception that PBL must be some huge, world-changing project that takes weeks, months, or even the entire school year. When we present and talk to teachers, we always get the question that everyone in the room is thinking, "Where do you find the time?" To this, we say, projects don't always have to be HUGE. Some projects we do in our classroom take only a few class periods. It might not check off every box of the essential elements of PBL, but what we always ask ourselves is, "Is this deeper learning than reading a textbook passage and taking a quiz?" When I find the answer is "yes," I go for it. Yes, Project-Based Learning takes more time, but it might not be as much time as you think.

Project-Based Learning shouldn't be looked at as one more thing on your plate. PBL should be a way of looking at what we are already doing and doing it more effectively. Yes, maybe we won't get through all twenty-four chapters of the social studies textbook, but the many we do get through and experience will have a much deeper impact than rushing through it all. All the clichés are true! You have to go slow to go fast. We'd rather teach an inch of content a mile deep than going only an inch deep and a mile wide. Basically, amazing things are possible when you give people time and get out of their way.

One of the best videos we've ever seen to demonstrate this process is called "Creativity Requires Time." We highly recommend you look up this video and show it during a staff meeting. In the video, students are asked to draw a clock in ten seconds. At the end of ten seconds, all of the clocks look very similar, and no real creativity is demonstrated. The next example is the same class with the same task; however, they are instead given ten minutes for their drawings. Each one is unique and creative in its own way.

https://youtu.be/WDngw5R32WE

The Lie: Project-based Learning is Easy!

If an outsider walked into our classrooms during the creation phase of a project, they might think it was pure chaos. I'll never forget one moment early on our PBL journey when Grayson and I were co-teaching. For a second, we just sat back for a minute and looked around in exhausted disbelief. We saw one group creating a keynote presentation, one group doing voice-overs in an iMovie project, two groups outside with the student teacher filming tutorials on how to play Native American Games, two groups were in the computer lab creating a PowToon video or an Adobe Spark website. One group was in the library with thirty-seven pencils taping them together and using butcher paper to create "fishing poles," "war hammers," and "bow and arrows" to demonstrate their learning.

The real moment of validation came when students told us they were meeting together on an upcoming half-day of school to work on their projects. We didn't assign homework; we didn't tell them to work on it at home. They did it purely because they wanted to.

While it may have looked chaotic, it was also pure engagement, collaboration, communication, and creativity all in action at the same time.

When we announced it was time for recess, students were disappointed and asked if they could continue working. I repeat, students were *disappointed* that social studies was over and it was time for recess! This was when we realized what real learning looks like...it's loud, it's messy, it's creative, and it's a beautiful sight!

THIS IS WHEN WE REALIZED WHAT REAL LEARNING LOOKS LIKE; IT'S LOUD, IT'S MESSY, IT'S CREATIVE, AND IT'S A BEAUTIFUL SIGHT!

#ExpertEffectEDU

13 TECHNOLOGY'S ROLE IN PROJECT-BASED LEARNING

> *Technology is just a tool. In terms of getting the kids working together and motivating them, the teacher is the most important.*

> —BILL GATES

This might be the most important sentence written in this book. Are you ready for it?

Are you sure?
Drumroll, please......
Repeat after us:
TECHNOLOGY IS A TOOL, NOT A LEARNING OUTCOME.

I think it's important to share my (Zach's) journey with technology to start off this chapter. A little backstory is that I was hired in 2013 on the third day of the school year in my dream district. I remember this being one of the happiest days of my life...quickly followed by an "Oh no, what-did-I-just-get-myself-into?" feeling as I walked in for my first official day of teaching on the second week of the school year. It's common to think that every teacher coming out of college is knowledgeable about technology and eager to use it. Well, let me tell you, this was not the case for me.

My college prep program did not do much to prepare us for how to use technology effectively in the classroom. (It didn't help that I took the technology course four years before graduating. We all know how much can change in just four years...I mean, I learned how to build a "Web-Quest" in that class.)

Within that first month of teaching, I would discover that we had an iPad cart with a class set of iPads that teachers could check out at the school. In that first year, I checked the iPad cart out a grand total of ZERO times.

I was terrified of the iPads. My students knew how to use them better than I did, so how could I teach them anything they didn't already know? I didn't know how to use them effectively, so I didn't even try. Although I may have only been 23 years old, I was still a classic techno-phobe at the helm of the classroom.

In the spring of my first year, we received an email from the district informing us that through the approval of a bond initiative, the next year, we would be going 1:1 with iPads for grades 3–8. It was time to face my fear.

Once I received my teacher iPad, I went all out with it. That summer, I downloaded many apps, played with new programs, read books and blogs on how I should integrate these new tools, followed many new people on Twitter, and experimented while teaching during summer school.

In my second and third years, I went off the deep end with technology. I was using technology for everything I could. I completed a master's degree in educational technology. I was presenting with Grayson to our staff, peers around the district, and at local conferences about all the cool new apps I found.

Looking back, I can say I learned a lot through this process and recognize that I made many, many mistakes in this process. But the biggest mistake I made in my first few years was putting technology in front of the learning outcomes. I was finding apps and stretching to use them in my classroom. While these new apps definitely got students excited, they didn't always line up with the content I was teaching or the outcomes I was looking to achieve.

I wasn't planning lessons backward with the end in mind. As educators, we all know we do not have any time in the day to waste just to use technology for technology's sake; it must be meaningful. It must have a purpose behind it. The key is to start with the *learning outcomes* and think about how you can leverage technology to help you get to the learning objective better.

I don't have an exact number or statistic to quantify it, but I can absolutely say that I used technology much less in my seventh year of teaching than in my second or third. The difference is that now, my use of technology is much more strategic, planned, and purposeful to create deeper learning opportunities for my students.

One model to conceptualize this idea is based on the SAMR model, created by Dr. Reuben Puentedura. This schema describes four levels of technology integration for schools. If you've never heard about this, we recommend checking it out. Essentially, it is a hierarchy of technology use that starts at the bottom with Substitution. This is when technology is used as a direct substitute with no functional improvement to its paper-pencil counterpart. The next stage is Augmentation, in which technology is a substitution, but has a functional improvement (think spell-check on Word or Google Docs instead of just paper and pencil).

As we move up the ladder to the next two levels, we start to see the magic happen. In the levels of Modification and Redefinition, we get to the point where we are giving students learning opportunities that would otherwise not be possible without technology.

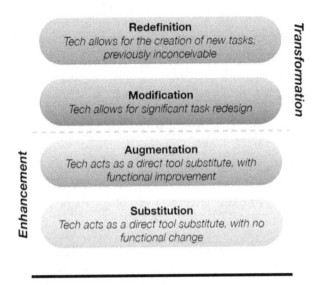

Credit: Dr. Ruben Puentedura

With the *Expert Effect* model, we aim to use technology to do three things:

1. Connect students with experts to learn from real-life sources

2. As a research tool for students to learn and become an expert in their research topic

3. To help students share their learning with an authentic and global audience that reaches far outside of the four walls of our classrooms

These aims would be nearly impossible without the use of certain technologies and move learning experiences to the transformational side of the SAMR Model.

14 PBL: JUST DO IT

 The great aim of education is not knowledge but action.

–HERBERT SPENCER

Project-Based Learning is when we as teachers can truly become the facilitators of learning instead of just the storehouse of facts to pass onto students. The best projects connect the students' learning to their world and aim to solve authentic and meaningful problems. We've found that the best PBL work in our classrooms has not come from intricate planning months in advance, but more like jumping down the rabbit hole of something that comes up organically during the school year.

Here's one morsel of positive feedback from the "feel-good" folder...from an inspired Twitter follower that our class received upon seeing the end product of a six-week session of Project-Based Learning in our classroom:

Inspiring change is so powerful. Letting them pursue their own ideas, collecting evidence, and communicating their solutions and recommendations is sooo awesome!!! Tell your students they are excellent forward thinkers and not to slow down their innovative thoughts!!! (Joanne Weatherby, 2019)

Let us give you an example of when we might seize an opportunity spontaneously to take to the next level. Every year as we begin our 4th-grade study of our state, we study Michigan's Tourism Industry. We have students pick a location in Michigan that is special to them, and they create their own Pure Michigan Commercial to match the advertising campaign in our state. This project includes social studies concepts with the study of tourism, math with budgeting, and persuasive writing through the production of a commercial script.

In 2019, our team was getting ready to launch this project again when we saw on the news that our governor, Gretchen Whitmer, had threatened to veto the budget for this advertising campaign after 10 successful years. If this plan were to go through, the Pure Michigan campaign would essentially be shut down and ended. Immediately, this struck me as an opportunity for an authentic learning experience that tied directly to our curriculum.

I showed my students the article the next day, and the debate began. We dove down the rabbit hole. We spent class time researching the impact of Michigan's tourism industry, the impact the Pure Michigan Campaign had had, and formed conclusions on whether we believed the campaign was worth the $36,000,000 that had been budgeted for it.

The real power of this project came in when we told students that if we wanted to make a difference in our world, then we would need to share our voices publicly on the issue. We were in an essay writing unit, so we combined our research and newly acquired persuasive writing skills to write letters to our state representative. We had students on both sides of the debate, and it was up to them to form their own opinion and share it with the world.

To take this one step further, we used technology to amplify our voices even more. We created a plan for a podcast episode, in which each student would write their unique script, and then we would publish our first episode of the year of our classroom podcast. Students' voices and opinions did not just live in our classroom anymore. Their learning and their voices were out in the world. Their learning was public and on display for the world to see. (Search 4th-Grade Innovators Podcast on any of the major podcast platforms and look for Season 2 Episode 1: The Pure Michigan Debate.)

Just a month after this, we had our annual field trip to the state Capitol Building in Lansing, Michigan. We were fortunate enough to be greeted by the same state representative we had written to just weeks before. She was in the process of dropping off a bill and explained to our class how a bill becomes a law (way more authentic to see her handing the bill off to someone as opposed to just reading about it in a textbook). Before she left, she asked if anyone had any questions. I must say, she seemed quite surprised when hands shot up, and fourth-graders started asking about the budget cuts to the Pure Michigan Campaign and the rationale behind the decision. This is one moment as a teacher that I will never forget.

If you give Project-Based Learning a try, you will likely see your students get excited about learning again. You will see your students work together with their classmates toward common goals. You will see your students struggle and fight through challenging learning moments. You will see your students become leaders and push their classmates to succeed. You will see them reflect on what worked, what didn't, and what they would do differently next time. Above all, you will see your students LEARN. As a teacher, when we see our students learning, excitement is contagious, and our creative spark continues well beyond the classroom—well beyond the school day. This makes it all worthwhile in the end. When it comes to innovation in education, there is no finish line...so JUST DO IT!

A PBL Success Story

If you're still not convinced about trying Project-Based Learning in your classroom, we have one story that will always stand out in our memory. As mentioned earlier, in the 2016–17 school year, Grayson and I teamed up and opened the wall in our classroom to create a "Learning Lab" for the year with fifty-six fourth graders and two teachers. This is when we really dove head-first into Project-based Learning.

We had done a few rounds of social studies projects, so the routine was familiar. Now, we like to joke about the War of 1812 and how memorizing the facts and dates of it should never really be the aim of education...nevertheless, it was one of the topics that a group of two students was studying. The two boys approached us to ask if they could remake the board game *Settlers of Catan* into a new version called *Settlers of the War of 1812*. Now let me tell you, I (Zach) knew NOTHING about this game (Grayson is the board game geek between the two of us) or how it could serve an educational purpose, but our answer was an immediate "yes!" We had never seen these two students work harder on something than they did on this project. They were going to each other's houses after school to create new rules, modify game pieces, and design a new deck of cards to teach about the content. They created unique scenarios from events from the War of 1812 and turned it into a game using the original tiles from *Catan*.

When it came down to the day of their presentation, they divided the class into teams and ran a full-blown board game/simulation with fifty-four other students like we had never seen. The entire class was engaged and learning about history through their creation. After a half hour of playing, it was time for recess, and there was an audible groan because the students did not want to stop playing. A group of about twenty students stayed in during recess to continue playing this game. We repeat, twenty students stayed in...from recess...to learn about the War of 1812! #ProudTeacherMoment

We don't share this story to say that all projects will end this way, but this was an important realization for us in the sense that sometimes as teachers, we just have to get out of the way and let students' creativity shine. We think back on this and how easy it would have been to let fear take over and turn their idea down because we didn't know how a popular game could turn educational. Sometimes students come to us as experts in their own ways. They bring with them a set of valuable experiences, insights, and opinions that deserve to be recognized and shared. We have to acknowledge their passions and skill sets and occasionally set aside our own agendas, and be willing to let them take the lead. This memory will forever stand out in our minds as a true success story with PBL.

SOMETIMES AS TEACHERS, WE JUST HAVE TO GET OUT OF THE WAY AND LET STUDENTS' CREATIVITY SHINE.

#ExpertEffectEDU

Safety Nets for Success

Student-driven Project-Based Learning does not mean total anarchy in the classroom. Well, honestly, it kind of did feel like that at first, but we have come up with some strategies to improve academic outcomes in any classroom (and prevent your classroom from being completely upended in the process). In this section, we share some strategies to help you maintain control over the classroom and keep your own sanity in the process.

Start with Immersion

By far, the most frequent questions and pushback we get on these ideas come from a place where teachers feel like they have to "stop teaching" and just let students "go." At first, this was the impression of PBL we had too, and it's an extremely uncomfortable thought. As teachers, we are led to believe that we have to be the driver of our students' learning and therefore, it does not feel good just saying "Okay, go!" to a class of nine-year-olds.

Fortunately, merely adopting an attitude of laissez-faire in the classroom is not what it takes to give students ownership over their learning (unless you actually do want anarchy in your classroom). Teachers still do and always will play a big part in conveying knowledge to their students. There's a narrative we've seen going around the Twitterverse lately that seems to be calling for the "death of the lecture." And while we agree that 100% lecture-driven classes where students simply "sit and get" should not be the *only* way students learn, story-telling is an essential part of education and culture. The art of storytelling has been ingrained in humanity for tens of thousands of years—at one time serving as the only form of teaching and learning. We know the power a good story can hold; our own students are very engaged when we are telling them a story from our personal lives that relates to the subject we're teaching.

But as with most things in life, moderation is key. Anytime teachers find themselves going to extremes, whether it's "100% lecture style" or "I don't talk to students, I just let them learn" approach, they are missing some key learning opportunities. The key with the lecture style is to keep it short. Pack them in ten- to fifteen-minute mini-lessons. As elementary teachers, we can see first-hand that students' attention spans are getting shorter and shorter. Tell stories, connect with students, pick a specific teaching point or two, deliver the content, and then allow students to practice the skill and experience the information for themselves. Immersion is about teaching enough to spark the curiosity within students, giving them enough information to spark the hunger to explore more, then giving them the opportunity to geek out over it and discover new information on their own. This kind of teaching and learning is like choreographing a dance—receiving, exploring, creating, transmitting— 1, 2, 3, 4.

Students can't create a project to share with others if they don't first have background information on the topic. At the start of any unit, the teacher's job is to immerse students in the topic and, most importantly, to get students passionately curious. Immersion can take place in many ways:

- Short mini-lessons of direct instruction
- Intriguing video clips from reputable sources
- Nonfiction articles and reading from collections of books
- Skyping with an expert to learn more

Once the class has created a shared basic understanding, it's time to let students move on to finding out more information about an aspect of a topic that is especially interesting to them.

Sorting Students by Interest, Not Friendships

Let us tell you our number one rookie mistake in an attempt to be the "cool teachers:" letting students pick their own groups. We should have filmed this process as a social experiment because in case you didn't already know, friends do not always make the best group members. When you let students choose groups, there are also always children to whom no one gravitates and you, as the teacher, have to put them in a group. This is an uncomfortable, "last-one-picked-for-dodgeball" type feeling we never want a student to feel.

We have found that it is much more effective to assign all students to groups in a way that still honors their choice in the process. Here's an example: to start our social studies projects, we give a survey that lists big ideas from the unit. We tell students to choose the top three topics they would like to study deeper. We guarantee them they will get one of their top three, but ultimately, we sort students into groups that we think will work best. Sorting students by interest and not friendships guarantees interest and engagement in the project while avoiding the pitfalls of working with the people who will distract and detract from the learning.

Another question we've often been asked deals with the "leveling" within groups. Is it better to group high achievers together and leave the rest to fend for themselves? Will students get more out of the experience by working with students of similar ability? No! We believe that keeping groups homogeneous is not beneficial for anyone. Creating groups of mixed abilities gives students the chance to learn from each other. Additionally, research done by Gene V. Glass of Arizona State University shows that pupils are at reduced risk of being stigmatized and exposed to a "dumbed-down" curriculum when matched with differently-abled peers. Furthermore, teachers' expectations for all pupils are maintained at higher levels. And finally, more opportunities exist for students to assist their peers in learning along the way (Glass, n.d.).

Group Constitutions

The first step in any successful group project is setting up group norms or rules to follow. To be honest, in fourth and fifth grade, students often have strong opinions about how they want their project to go and aren't very willing to see things from others' perspectives. Rather than letting this discourage us from doing group projects, we look at these as teachable moments to work through the problems and find an agreeable solution. We did mention that teachers wear a lot of hats, and being a professional mediator is definitely one of them! Tie these constitutions back to the mission statement or values vision of the class. For us, that means reminding students that we will be using our learning to improve our own lives, the lives of others, and the world around us. Having group norms to refer back to when disagreements come up is always helpful in solving the problem and finding common ground.

Group Check-Ins

It can get really easy during a project to spend more time with certain groups and forget to check in with others. One of the worst feelings is to realize that as a project's time frame is winding down that a group in your class has accomplished virtually nothing. This can be avoided by having scheduled check-ins with every group. You can set this up in various ways—walking around with a clipboard and marking off when you check in or giving groups a "checkpoint" where they have to meet with you when they reach a certain point in the process.

One way we tried this while co-teaching was to create a very basic SMART Board file with each group numbered and the stages of the project at the top. After sorting students into groups based on interest, each group started in the first column: the "brainstorming phase." As groups progressed, they moved their number to the next phase in the process. In the graphic below, you will see that we scheduled two "teacher conferring" stages where students were required to meet with one of us before moving on to the next step. This was the most effective way we found to ensure that we checked in with every group to provide feedback and guidance throughout the PBL process before too much time had slipped away. Using a check-in chart like this made it super simple to see at a glance, even from far across the room, who needed to be nudged along, who needed immediate assistance, and who was ready to be given an extra challenge.

Brainstorming	Researching	Teacher Conferring	Working on Final Product	Teacher Conferring	Ready to Showcase!
			Group 2	Group 6	Group 1
		Group 5	Group 3	Group 4	
			Group 7		

Reflection on the Process

 We do not learn from experience…

we learn from reflecting on experience.

–JOHN DEWEY

Oftentimes, we spend so much time on the projects themselves that when we're done, we feel we need to immediately move on to the next unit. We have certainly been guilty of the "on to the next" mentality many times over. One thing the formal PBL training teaches you is that the reflection piece is actually the most important. In creating a project, students just went on a journey. They started with little knowledge on the subject, but ended up with a website, a movie, or a skit that they created with their new knowledge. It's important we prompt students to reflect, celebrate, and be proud of their accomplishments. Reflection can take place in many ways. The prompts below could be used in a written format, a class discussion, a group conference, or in an individual video reflection. The power of reflection isn't about the format it's completed in, it's about the thinking it sparks.

Sample Reflection Questions:

- What parts of the project were successful?
- What are you proud of?
- When did you struggle, and what did you learn from it?
- What do you know now that you didn't know before?
- If you could do this assignment over, what would you do differently?
- What advice would you give someone doing this assignment next year?
- What resources did you learn the most from?
- Why is it important to learn this information?
- How did your group work together as a team?

PART II: THINK + TWEET

#ExpertEffectEDU

1. In what area of your existing curriculum do you think you can incorporate more Project-Based Learning?
2. What projects do you remember from your own experiences as a student? What made them memorable, and how might you recreate that same feeling for the students you currently serve?
3. What excites you about the idea of Project-Based Learning?
4. If you use Project-Based Learning already, what has been your most successful project? What made it successful?
5. What product can students create to showcase their learning? (blog, website, live skit, Keynote/PowerPoint presentation, iMovie, board game, eBook, writing a song, etc...)

PART III
TEACH OTHERS AS EXPERTS

15 THE POWER OF THE "PLATFORM"

> *When students are sharing their work with the world, they want it to be good. When they are just sharing it with you, they want it to be good enough.*

-RUSHTON HURLEY

I t all started with student voice. In the summer of 2016, we rolled out a new professional learning presentation called "Speak Up & Be Heard: Amplifying Student Voice." We traveled to conferences all around our state, sharing our passion for making sure we were letting students share their voices in various ways. Our goal was to help teachers far and wide to empower their most disenfranchised learners by raising up their voices.

Of course, we want our students to feel they have a voice and input into our own classrooms. Still, after speaking on this topic for a while, we realized we only had half of the equation right…capturing students' voices is essential, but the way to truly amplify this is to help students build an authentic global audience. We created the "*Expert Effect* Theorem" to explain this concept mathematically.

STUDENT VOICE + AUTHENTIC AUDIENCES = MIND-BLOWING, EARTH-SHATTERING LEARNING EXPERIENCES!

#ExpertEffectEDU

Mathematically speaking, we have found when you take your students' voice, add in an authentic, global audience, the result is mind-blowing, earth-shattering learning experiences for our students. They see themselves as people who can affect change in the world...that they are a part of the conversation, with ideas and beliefs to contribute!

If we are being honest, this is our favorite part of the *Expert Effect* model. This is where we truly see students' love of learning come alive. Once students gain expertise on a subject, it's time we turn it over to them and give them a platform and an opportunity to share their expertise with the world. PBLWorks calls this aspect of the process the "Public Product." We truly believe this is where the learning becomes "cemented" and where engagement and excitement for a project multiply.

When we expect students to share their learning on more than just a formal test, it raises the bar and puts a little bit of pressure on them. When they have to share their findings, they are going to make sure they know their stuff and can back up their claims. When they know people will question them, they will want to make sure they know the answers.

We compare this feeling to when we go to a conference or workshop and know that when we return to our district, we will be responsible for sharing out at the next staff meeting. When this is the case, we make sure we are fully paying attention and learning the material well enough to teach others. There's a quote from Albert Einstein that goes something like this: "If you can't explain something simply, you don't know it well enough." When students have to teach their content to others, they learn it well enough to teach it simply. When students have to take a multiple-choice test, they remember the content only until it's no longer needed.

At one point in time, it was pretty important to have a healthy dose of fear in order to survive the harshness of a prehistoric world. Without fear, one might have casually waltzed up to a saber-toothed tiger to pet the "pretty kitty" and have been devoured in the process. Today, however, for better or worse, the number one fear of the modern *Homo sapien* is, to some degree, one of the imagined judgments from one's peers. The more authentic the audience, the more our students sense the significance of their works, and the more effort they put into making them great.

While raising the stakes can sometimes be a great motivating factor, we want to be careful not to add too much pressure on our students. But, when we are able to show students that the people will see their work, hear their words, and learn from their creations actually *care* about the *quality* of their content, then we can get students to amp up the level of their work. This taps into students' feeling of pride and motivates them to put out the best product they can to the world.

Think about it. How do you feel when you're writing a text message to your teaching partner or a friend? For me (Zach), I don't proofread, I don't format it; I just type and fire it off. But now, think of a time you have had to send your entire school an email about something you are in charge of. I know when I do this, I read and re-read, proofread, and edit so my message is perfectly clear and professional. Why is this? Because the audience matters!

We coined the term "selective perfectionism" to describe this feeling. This is the idea that when students are creating work just for the teacher or the class, they will put in just enough effort for it to be acceptable. However, when students publish a blog, a video, or a podcast episode, they know it will be consumed by a larger global audience. They now will no longer be content with "good enough" anymore. This ratchets up the pressure and turns them into selective perfectionists who only want their best work out in the world.

Our goal in giving students authentic audiences is not to encourage them to become a celebrity influencer who's looking for hearts, stars, and subscribers. We don't want to perpetuate the culture of a constant need for validation and likes from people on the internet. Instead, we want to teach them the value of building communities around the content they produce. Authentic audiences are key to getting kids to see themselves as experts who can positively affect the world.

So, you might be wondering, what exactly is an authentic audience? We're glad you asked. In short, we believe an authentic audience is anyone or any group of people with whom students are excited to share their work. An authentic audience is one who motivates students to do their best work because they know it will be viewed by this audience.

Example: I tell my students that they are going to turn their projects in to me, and I will take them home to show my parents their hard work. Authentic audience? No, not really.

Better example: We are going to start a classroom podcast, and it will be available on Apple Podcasts, Spotify, and ten other platforms. Students see that their podcasts and voices have been listened to in twenty-six different countries on four different continents, including Santiago, Anthony's uncle who lives in Spain, Saanvi, Ashwin's aunt who lives near New Delhi, and Emma, Kate's grand-mère who lives in France. Do you think that might get kids excited? You bet!

This is not to say that you must start a classroom podcast, but we feel like it's imperative to give students the chance to teach others as experts through some medium. Not only because of how it can affect their learning progress while in school, but because we believe that when they are given these chances year after year, it can help build the foundation of important life skills along with a deep love of learning. We want our students to earn the right to say with unabashed and unwavering confidence, "I can do difficult things." When we set them up with a task that will be shown to an authentic audience, we push them right to the edge of their comfort zone and beyond. It is at these moments that the brain is most unlocked and most alive. When we give children the chance to push themselves and explore their own limits, we are scaffolding them to go further than they ever thought possible. In the process, we help lay the groundwork, which builds confidence to take on even bigger challenges in the future.

As the larger-than-life Dave Burgess (@BurgessDave) says in *Teach Like a PIRATE*, "If you haven't failed in the classroom lately, you aren't pushing the envelope far enough. Safe lessons are a recipe for mediocrity" (Burgess, 2012, p. 48). If teachers aren't pushing themselves to go big, how can we ask students to do the same? When we are in these "deep waters," when we are at peak awareness and focus, truly alive in the moment. As Susan David, PhD says, "Discomfort is the price of admission to a meaningful life." It's time we started giving students these experiences that push the emotional envelope at an early age before the stakes are truly high, when we can create an arena for small failures, and perhaps more importantly, forums of feedback loops and the ability to reflect on their learning.

In short, we believe that it is the modern classroom teacher's job to ensure that the learning of their students doesn't lamely linger in the classroom...and *definitely* doesn't die on a worksheet. Give your students authentic audiences to push them to the edge of their comfort zone. It will increase the rigor of the learning activity, build relationships with classmates and interested individuals in the community at large, make the content more relevant to the lives of your students, and allow you to be amazed at the results they create!

GIVING STUDENTS AN AUTHENTIC AUDIENCE IS THE SECRET
SAUCE THAT INCREASES RIGOR, BUILDS RELATIONSHIPS,
MAKES CONTENT RELEVANT, AND GETS AWESOME RESULTS!

#ExpertEffectEDU

16 GROWING YOUR AUDIENCE: NEAR AND FAR

LEARN TO LIVE BY THE MENTALITY OF
"WHO CAN WE LEARN FROM, WHO CAN WE TEACH?"
#ExpertEffectEDU

Audiences Close to Home

Trying to recruit authentic audiences for your students may seem somewhat scary, but we promise it doesn't have to be. You don't have to start by publishing your students' work on the internet, creating a podcast or class blog. You can, and should, start small. The best place to start recruiting audiences within your own school—a very easy and effective way to start by looking for opportunities to give your students a wider audience. We break this section down into four different categories, each section ramping up the audience bit by bit.

Same-Aged Peers

From an elementary perspective, we find that as students spend their time with the same peers every day; they get more comfortable and complacent with the people in the class. To shake things up, it helps to invite other people in. This can be as simple as inviting another class from the same grade level to view presentations or share writing pieces. When students are getting ready to showcase their learning on a certain project, it can make a big difference just to invite the other classes in to view some of the group presentations.

Of course, we don't have the time to have sixty students sit through sixty different individual presentations—we feel anxious just picturing this—but we can set up showcases or do this in creative ways. You can pair children up with a student from another class or a small group of students and let them share their expertise that way. You can set up a miniature showcase where people walk around the room and talk to different students about their learning. The great part about this simple connection is that the other class is likely learning the same content, too, so they will be more interested to see how it connects and compares with their learning as well.

Different-Aged Peers

Another way to increase engagement is to invite classes from other grade levels in to view finished products. As fourth-grade teachers, we especially like inviting the third graders to see our projects which gives them a sneak peek of what they will be doing the following year. As an added bonus, it starts the relationship-building process months in advance, too! Older classes also always love going to see younger student's work and reminiscing about what they did with a similar project when they were in that grade.

Buddy Classes

At our school, each class has a corresponding buddy class, which is another great way to build relationships between older and younger kids and give students a special audience. Our buddy classes meet about once a month, and this allows them to get to know others in the school and become a "repeat customer" for seeing their work. The older students really relish this opportunity to be a role model to a younger student, who in turn looks up to their older buddies.

Whole-School Learning Showcases

When you're ready to step it up and want to showcase the learning of a big project, our go-to move has been to host whole-school learning fairs. For years, we hosted an Entrepreneur Day where students created their own mock business model and had to come up with Shark Tank-style pitches to present to the audience. The culmination of this project is setting up shop in the school cafeteria and inviting all the grades to come in for the big event.

Another example of getting the whole school involved is our Coding Expo, where students created an idea for an app and developed a proto-type for it by using Keynote. We invited the entire school to sign up for time slots to learn about students' apps and hear their presentations. We also have done this same setup for our Cardboard Challenge day as inspired by the viral short film, *Caine's Arcade*. (All of these projects are talked about in-depth in Part IV.)

When launching any of these particular projects, we make it a point to let them know up front that their work will be on display for the entire school. When students know this from the start, they work harder, so they don't have a sub-par product to show in front of the rest of the school. And in those rare (okay, sometimes often) times when students need a little extra motivation, it can go a long way to say, "Hey, you're going to have 300 other students coming to see your project on Friday. I would make sure you are focused and giving your best effort today."

Adults in the School

Another powerful way to boost excitement is to invite important adults into the presentations. We love inviting our principal into our celebra-tions and letting her give our classes feedback. Having frequently witnessed their creations, she is also able to talk to students about their projects and learning in the lunchroom and around the school later on, which in turn helps her build those deeper connections as well.

We are also lucky to have an extremely supportive superintendent, who, despite his busy schedule, is always looking to get into classrooms and see the learning process in our schools. Students get really excited and feel very important when these school leaders come in to see their learning. We also reach out to our school secretaries, cafeteria workers, board members, and other central office team members whenever possible to come to see our students' work as well.

When we value students' work to the point of inviting others in to see it, students get more engaged in the learning process. Engaged students are students who learn and remember what they learn, which is the ultimate goal.

So, our challenge to you is this: who in your immediate school setting can you recruit as an audience for your students? Now, it's time to start dreaming bigger and make the world your audience.

Growing a Global Audience

Go into any elementary classroom nowadays and ask the classic, "What do you want to be when you grow up?" question, and we can guarantee you'll hear at least a handful of students say they want to be a "YouTuber" or "eSports streamer." It's an easy gut reaction to want to fight this and say, "Be more realistic," but there's also a major opportunity here to tap into this "YouTube Effect" in schools. Why fight against students' passions when we can harness this by giving students a global audience to share their learning with?

Yes, as teachers, we like to think that our students appreciate and genuinely care about our feedback, and in most cases, they do. But do you think we compare to the idea of another individual across the world listening to a podcast or video blog entry our students have created and leaving a review on the site? Yeah, that's just way cooler than us.

In general, we've found that the bigger the audience, the greater the buy-in from students. We won't sugar coat it; this part isn't easy. It requires thought, planning, and execution. This isn't something to be done with every lesson, but when carefully implemented, it can truly change the culture of your classroom and get students excited about the possibilities within school.

We have found by using tools like Seesaw, Flipgrid, Twitter, student-created podcasts, and websites or blogs, we have been able to have our students' voices reach a global audience that would never have been possible without the use of technology.

Seesaw

I (Zach) first realized this lesson in my third year of teaching in a third-grade classroom. One morning, a student came running in ecstatically, and the conversation went like this:

Student: *"Mr. Rondot! Mr. Rondot! You'll never guess what happened last night."*

Me: *"Umm... What happened???"*

Student: *"My grandma called to tell me and she read my essay last night!"*

While this anecdote might not seem like a monumental revelation, the important part to know is that this student's grandmother lived in India. The night before, we had published our essays to Seesaw, and her father was able to share her writing with a link from Seesaw to his Facebook page for her family abroad to see. Yes, before this, they could have taken a picture and sent it to the grandmother, but the fact was they didn't. This was just after Seesaw had launched, so it was the first time something like this was really possible. I can tell you, it changed everything for this student to know her family, both near and far, would now readily be her audience.

During this same assignment, another one of my brilliant third graders wrote a heartfelt piece on the need to help all of the stray dogs of India. This was a big problem that she had noticed on her trip to visit her family the previous summer. Two girls in my class decided to team up and create an awareness campaign about this issue. This is where the learning took off, and I just had to get out of the way and encourage them. These students spent some time on their project during class, but mostly used their time at home to create a website and a series of PSA-style videos. Through Seesaw, they continued to communicate throughout the summer following third grade and kept taking action. They created a petition that went around the school, they held meetings, and they even planned a fundraiser.

While writing this book, I searched YouTube to see these videos again and found another video that had been published two years later for a project they were working on in the fifth grade. Seeing that this project continued to remain relevant in their lives even years later has made a huge impression on me. I was lucky to see a glimpse of the impact that my teaching had on them.

My point here is not that I did anything especially amazing as a teacher that drove this learning and their mission. I taught the writing unit, they picked the topic to write about and chose to make a website, create videos, and spread awareness. My role was simply to be their biggest cheerleader. While it started as nothing more than a school assignment, it turned into something much bigger. This further proves that when students produce work that taps into their passion and is made available to a global audience they care about, the learning doesn't die in the classroom. The learning lives on forever.

Flipgrid

Another app we love to use to get students' voices out to the wider world is Flipgrid. Flipgrid immediately taps into the "YouTube Effect" by having students record short videos and allowing other students to leave video replies. With some planning, you can use this tool to amplify student voices to audiences well outside the classroom.

We were first introduced to this idea when we played a game of Mystery Skype with a class in Florida. Mystery Skype is essentially a quick game of geographical 20 Questions to figure out where in the world the other class is located. This is fun on its own, but by connecting students on

Flipgrid after, they can continue to teach each other about their home locales. Some of the kids in Florida had never seen snow in person, so we opened our classroom door and filmed videos of our class playing in the snow. One student from Florida asked my students, "So do you always have to wear 'snow coats' in Michigan?" Thankfully, the answer is no, and students could respond with pictures of northern Michigan in its full summer glory.

Once we realized the potential of connecting students from different locations via Flipgrid, our minds started to percolate with ideas. We were just finishing up writing some informational books on the Civil War, so we had students create video versions of themselves reading their books and posted them to Flipgrid. We sent the grid link to another 4th-grade teacher in our district whose students were finishing the same project, and their class posted their books as well. Students were able to read each other's books from across town and leave comments for each other. The amazing thing was that that night, our email inboxes were blowing up with notifications that new videos were continuing to be posted from students reading and responding to others' books.

If we were to assign the homework, "Spend twenty minutes reading about the Civil War," we are quite confident that less than half of the class would have done this. But here, with an authentic audience, students voluntarily were reading and learning about the content we wanted them to.

Twitter

Another essential educational resource to get the students' message out to the world is Twitter. Both of us have been growing our professional learning networks since 2013. We can't even begin to quantify the impact of learning from the amazing educators around the world with whom we've connected. Twitter can be an amazing place to connect our students with real-world experts and give them an authentic audience for their work.

Each year, we both do many chapter book read-alouds to promote the love of reading with our students and to enjoy books together. One of my (Zach's) favorite series to read throughout the year is the *Poppy* series by Avi. Students are always so crushed at the end of the sixth book when the series comes to an end. One particular year, we were getting ready to start our author study unit, and I chose Avi since our class was already so invested in his writing.

As students were voicing their disappointment about not having another book in the series, I got an idea and ran with it without any real plan in mind. I immediately said, "Hey, if you want a seventh *Poppy* book so badly, then let's write up mini-stories that could continue the series, and we'll send them directly to Avi!" At this point, I had no idea how I would reach Avi, but the kids were PUMPED. Over the next weeks of the unit, students created unique storylines to continue the adventures in the woodland creatures' realm. We studied Avi's craft as an author to make it sound just right. We used the app Book Creator on our iPads to publish books and narrate them. We uploaded these videos to Flipgrid, and then came the moment of truth.

I pulled up my Twitter account in front of the class, and we composed a tweet to Avi:

Zach Rondot
@MrRondot

Dear @avi3writer. We loved the Poppy Series so much that we didn't want it to end! We decided to write the 7th book ourselves! Click the link below to see our ideas! We are 4th graders from MI & we hope you like what we came up with! -Mr. Rondot's Class
flipgrid.com/b27a0d

1:01 PM · Jun 11, 2018 · Twitter Web Client

Now trust me, at this point, I expected the project to end. I had motivated students all along by saying that Avi was going to read their books, but I can't really say I believed it. But then that night, I was working a little late and saw a notification appear on my phone. I opened Twitter to find:

Avi, writer
@avi3writer

Replying to @MrRondot

Dear class, Thanks for your ideas. I AM writing a new Poppy book. It will become the 2nd book in the series, telling the story of how Ragweed met Poppy. But writing and publishing take a long time. It will be at least a year before it's all ready. Hang in there. Your friend, Avi

6:05 PM · Jun 11, 2018 · Twitter Web Client

The next morning, instead of the interactive lunch and attendance board I usually project on the SMART Board each day, I had this tweet pulled up. Kids walked into class, looked to the board, and immediately began screaming. No, Avi didn't take one of my students' ideas and decide to write a new book, but to them, it was still huge! They heard from one of their idols and were able to see that he had read their books! Furthermore, Avi didn't announce this upcoming book on his blog or website until months after this, so as far as I'm concerned, we were the first people to hear about his new project!

On its own, this writing assignment would have been pretty cool. Students would have enjoyed creating these stories in any case. But what ramped this project up another notch was the idea that Avi himself was going to view their work. I had never seen these students so diligent about checking their grammar and punctuation as they were here because they didn't want a famous author to see any mistakes. Giving students an authentic audience that excites them takes student empowerment to the next level and provides an unmatched level of engagement in the learning process.

Part III: Think + Tweet

#ExpertEffectEDU

1. How do you empower students to find their own pathways now and in the future?
2. How do you create a culture in your school and classroom where you learn for, about, and with those you serve?
3. When do you create spaces for students to both lead and follow in learning?
4. Who in your immediate school setting can you recruit as an audience for your students? Who could you recruit from your central office? Local government?
5. In what ways can you give your students a global audience? Dream big!

PART IV

PUTTING IT ALL TOGETHER

17 EXAMPLES OF LEARNING WITH ALL THREE PARTS

> *It's not our future we are preparing students for, but theirs. We can ill afford to prepare them for a world that won't exist.*

–ERIC SHENINGER (@E_SHENINGER)

This was never meant to be a work of philosophy. We have lived and breathed and taught with the *Expert Effect* as our model for the last few years. The results of our shift in thinking about who we can get our kids to learn from, what we can have them create, and with whom they can share their new knowledge has transformed our classrooms from "sit and get" to "go out there and make it happen!" We want our students to always know that they have the ability to impact the world today—not in the future once they're "all grown up"—TODAY!

SCHOOL SHOULDN'T BE "SIT AND GET"...IT SHOULD BE "GO OUT AND MAKE IT HAPPEN!"
#ExpertEffectEDU

In this final section of our book, we'll put it all together for you, showing what a transformative difference the *Expert Effect* can make, with examples from our experiences and those of some of our colleagues.

Podcasting in the Classroom: A Tale of Two Casts

By far, the most extreme and exciting example of us giving our students a global audience was by starting classroom podcasts to give our students a platform to share their learning with the world. Here are two different takes on a similar idea.

The 4th-Grade Innovators Podcast

The Story

I (Zach) shared earlier in the book that I had the opportunity to attend a two-day training on Project-based Learning from the Buck Institute (PBL Works) in the summer of 2018. As I mentioned, this training changed the way I approach teaching and learning.

I went through this training as part of a two-year teacher leadership program called the Galileo Teacher Leadership Consortium. This was not just a one-and-done type of training. We were challenged to come up with a big project that we would tackle in the upcoming school year.

An idea popped into my head...*I want to start a classroom podcast.*

I'm an avid podcast listener and have learned so much through podcasts, so I knew it could be a valuable tool, and students would love becoming "podcasters." But quickly, fear took over...

"Who am I to make a podcast?"

"I'm not an expert; I don't even know how."

"You've gone too far this time, Zach. Next idea..."

So, I listened to my internal critic and spent the next two days planning a social studies project—one that I felt more comfortable with. (I actually planned for what would later become the Pure Michigan Project, also mentioned in this book, so it wasn't a total loss.)

But as I teach my students, great things never come from staying in our comfort zones. As the beginning of the next school year approached, this idea of a podcast kept popping up in my head over and over again. So, I decided to put the pressure on myself, to stop playing small, and to make it happen. Approximately twelve minutes before parents entered my room for Curriculum Night, where I was to share my grand vision for the year, I inserted a slide into my presentation and just wrote: "Classroom Podcast!" I explained to parents that this was an idea I had but that I had no idea how to pull it off yet. I asked them to not tell the students yet, and I would keep them posted.

Now, this is where the story gets really interesting. Sitting in my car getting ready to drive home that very night, I opened the podcast app on my phone to find a new episode from my favorite series, *The Wired Educator Podcast*. The new episode was titled, "Everyone Can Create Podcasts" and was a complete tutorial on starting a podcast with students. The "Wired Educator," Kelly Croy, had come to my rescue!

I listened, learned, and played with the tools and software. I discovered Anchor.fm, an extremely easy platform for publishing podcasts. Luckily, I already had a quality microphone I had purchased with a grant the previous school year, so I was ready to roll.

But, I had one more thought. I didn't want to just explain this idea to my students and present it as my idea. I wanted them to have some ownership over it as well. So, I started playing podcasts like *Wow in the World, Brains On!,* and *Tumble* during science lessons. During our morning meeting, when my students were discussing wise words quotes, I kept saying things like, "Wow! These are such brilliant thoughts; I wonder if there's a way you could teach others."

And then, it happened. The moment I was waiting for. As we finished listening to a science episode, a student said, "Mr. Rondot, do you think we could make a podcast?"

"I don't know, class. What do you think?" I asked. They all shouted back, "Yes! Can we?" So, I ditched the math lesson that day, and we spent the next thirty minutes in complete brainstorming mode of why we should start a podcast, what we would talk about, what subjects we could teach, and so on. I cut off the discussion, and we made no final decisions. I just told them to think about it more that night, and we would continue the conversation the next day. Soon after, the *4th-Grade Innovators Podcast* was born!

I have to say, this has been the most exciting project I have done in my eight years of teaching so far. One of the biggest lessons I've learned from it is that magic happens when you bring your personal passions into the classroom.

As I mentioned, I am a huge podcast junkie and listen to them all the time. This was motivating for me and exciting to move from consumer to creator. Students pick up on our energy more than we probably think. When we as teachers get excited and passionate about something, that energy and emotion is transferred directly to the students, resulting in high engagement learning. As educator Haim Ginott of Columbia University once said of the teacher's role in the classroom, "It's my personal approach that creates the climate. It's my daily mood that makes the weather. As a teacher, I possess a tremendous power to make a child's life miserable or joyous. I can be a tool of torture or an instrument of inspiration." We don't need to tell you which of these directions should be your aim.

Throughout the process of creating The *4th-Grade Innovators Podcast*, we used *The Expert Effect* formula to learn from experts, become experts, and teach the world like experts too.

Here is a video about the entire process of creating the *4th-Grade Innovators Podcast,* along with the voices of my students and their perspective.

https://www.youtube.com/watch?v=_l7YazPkHwI

Driving Question:

How can we use technology to positively impact the world?

Learn From Experts:

The reality of this was that I had no idea how to start a podcast, how to promote it, or how to make sure it wouldn't die after a few episodes. One way for all of us to learn about podcasting was to learn from a real-world expert. I contacted Kelly Croy, host of the *Wired Educator* and *Future Focused* podcasts. He taught us many lessons from how to use an interesting and dramatic voice, how often we should make episodes, the importance of having a consistent format, and how to respond if we were to ever get negative feedback with putting our work out to the world.

Become the Experts through Project-Based Learning:

Intentionally, we did a lot of work before starting to record. I really wanted to convey that if students wanted to be podcasters, we had to become experts on our subject matter first. We did a lot of brainstorming on topics, and ultimately, we wanted to extend the positivity and discussions from our daily morning meeting and amplify those messages out to the world. We wanted to inspire and motivate people from all around the world. Students learned about these topics during our meeting and then researched topics like growth mindset, positivity, mindfulness, goal setting, and more to create their scripts.

Teach Others as Experts:

Now, this is the part where true magic occurred during this project. When we finally got our first episodes recorded and edited, it was time to publish. As a class, we were so excited. Deep down, I must admit that I was a little scared too. I hoped people would listen.

I promoted this and announced it via Twitter and what happened next, I don't think any of us expected. Within the first week, we had ninety downloads and received messages from teachers in Africa, Asia, Europe, and all over the United States and Canada. We were making an impact and spreading our message to classrooms all over the world!

At the time of this writing, our podcast has been listened to over 3,300 times from thirty-one different countries around the world. This is what really drove the whole process—the fact that students had an authentic audience to teach and share their ideas with. Without a wide audience, I'm sure this still would have been an exciting process, but the fact that it kept growing is what kept students excited. In this first year, we created nine episodes. We have continued this into a second season and hopefully many more.

We would be honored if you listened at anchor.fm/4thgradeinnovators or downloaded on any major podcast platform!

anchor.fm/4thgradeinnovators

The 5th-Grade Futurists Podcast

The Story:

To this day, I feel that the most inspirational and career-changing thing that happened to me was co-teaching with Zach. That year will always be remembered as a turning point on which I shifted from being a teacher who taught the curriculum, to being one who taught the children in front of me. When I saw what kind of impact Zach was having on his kids' enthusiasm for the subject-matter, I knew I had to follow suit. I began thinking of ways in which we could incorporate podcasting into what we were already doing as well.

We had just finished a writing unit on journalism, in which we experimented with mixing narrative and essay-style writing in order to report on current events that had been happening around our school. The next bend of the unit was going to take us deeper into the genre and look at how journalists wrote in-depth articles, as opposed to stories that merely cover the 5 Ws (who, what, when, where, and why). It was then that the creative juices got flowing, and I saw the angle we were meant to take.

For a long while, I had been in awe of Australian teacher and thought-leader Bronwyn Joyce (@JoyceBronwyn). At the time of this journalism project, she had just introduced me to the United Nations 17 Global Goals for a Sustainable Future. These Sustainable Development Goals (SDGs) were the perfect subject matter for my class to investigate and write about. A school-wide newspaper wasn't going to cut it, though, if we were going to truly raise awareness around the world of ways in which we could improve the planet and ensure a future that is healthy, safe, and fair for all. Enter the *5th-Grade Futurists Podcast.*

Driving Question:

How can we use what we know about writing strong journalism articles in order to raise awareness of the United Nations 17 Global Goals for a Sustainable Future?

Learn From Experts:

I am most proud of how we enlisted help from multiple experts in the field to gain tips and insights about making our journalism writing better and more interesting. We first reached out to experts close to home. We invited Kerry Birmingham, an Emmy Award-winning journalist, turned school district strategic communications director, to come in for a talk. Next, we reached out to in-depth columnists at The Detroit Free Press and The Detroit News. In later years, we were also able to connect with the Pulitzer Center for Journalism and Education, and through their line-up of award-winning journalists from around the world, Skyped with NPR's Rebecca Hersher and TheGrio.com's Natasha Alford to ask them about their experiences in the field. From all of these experts, we gained invaluable insights and memorable conversations, all of which helped us to understand the importance of and skills needed to be a journalist.

Become Experts through Project-Based Learning:

Students wrote articles on an SDG that mattered to them and then collaborated with others in the class to transform what they had written into a script to broadcast. We took these scripts to the workshop to edit and revise, jumping back-and-forth between learning from and becoming, by studying how other podcasts typically went. We found that in order to make our shows not only informative but also entertaining, we had to tap into our creativity and showmanship, making an attention-grabbing and compelling argument for caring about the issues outlined in the Global Goals. Eventually, we also took these scripts into our "recording studio," a setup in our classroom that included two microphones on booms and a laptop that were purchased with the help of an educational grant. We taped a sign to our classroom door that read, "Recording in Progress," and we were off!

Teach Others as Experts:

The beauty of creating a classroom podcast is that, like a website, it's an ongoing platform for sharing the content created by your class. You can plan for it to be as long- or short-lived as you want, although if your kids are anything like ours, they will want it to continue for as long as they are your students! I had only intended to make this podcast last for the duration of our journalism unit in writing, but like so many Project-based Learning experiences, it took on a life of its own. While the original goal was to publish five episodes in five weeks, we ended up producing twelve original episodes. Our students couldn't get enough and wanted to create a brand new script every time we came across an interesting article in the news or in our social studies textbook. Not only had I taught them the basics of journalistic writing (with outside expert help), but I also had turned them into journalists, looking for stories everywhere they went. It was a magical experience, and wouldn't have been possible if we didn't live by the mentality of "Who can we learn from, who can we teach?"

We, too, would be honored if you listened at anchor.fm/thefuturist5 or downloaded an episode on any major podcast platform! In this way, YOU will be the "others" that we teach.

anchor.fm/thefuturist5

The Pure Michigan Campaign

The Story:

The fourth-grade curriculum in our district is a full-year study of our state, and we always like to launch into this by starting with a short PBL unit on Michigan's tourism industry. Here, we have an incredible campaign called #PureMichigan, which attempts to spread messages of Michigan's beautiful attractions to get more people to visit our great state. Even if you aren't from Michigan, you may have seen the iconic Pure Michigan commercials voiced by Tim Allen. We see and hear them a lot in our state, but they also play in other states to try to convince people to visit Michigan. Tourism is an extremely important industry in Michigan, so this project highlights its importance and concludes with students creating their own Pure Michigan campaign commercials.

Driving Question:

How does the tourism industry in Michigan affect the economy?

Learn From Experts:

During this project, we could have just read the prescribed pages out of our ancient textbook and learned that yes, people do like to come to Michigan in the summer because of the miles and miles of sandy beaches along the Great Lakes and in the winter for the snow fun up north. It would have been easy enough, right? But no, tourism is such a huge part of our state we felt it should be a deeper lesson than just a simple "read and forget."

From a simple Google search, I found the contact information for those who worked on the Pure Michigan campaign team, and I sent out a few emails. I did not receive a response from the first few emails, but on my fifth try, I got ahold of a gracious member of the team, Ken Yaesevich, an advertising specialist, who was willing to Skype with our class.

This experience completely blew my expectations out of the water. My class and I got so much out of this exchange, and we learned so much about the entire process of creating the Pure Michigan promotions. Ken taught us that it takes approximately six months to create each 30-

second commercial, that they almost called this campaign, "Find Your True North," and that Michigan receives $8 in return for every $1 spent on this ad campaign. After the video call, his office even mailed us an entire set of their Winter Pure Michigan Winter Magazines, so we could study their print advertisements as well. (Talk about a good ROI.)

Become Experts through Project-Based Learning:

The fact is my students became hooked; they wanted to learn more. To end this unit, students had to pick a specific place in Michigan, research the place extensively, and create their own Pure Michigan Ad convincing people to come to visit their location. They had to include entertainment ideas for each season and for different budgets, including free things to do too.

Teach Others as Experts:

In the end, when all students finished their commercials, we held a movie viewing party, complete with popcorn, to celebrate their hard work. Ken had asked us to send him our videos so his team could watch them. Do you think students were even more motivated knowing the producers of the actual commercials were going to watch theirs? You bet!

Cross-curricular Connections:

Social Studies, Writing, and Math: Students extensively studied and learned about Michigan's tourism industry. They learned the effects it has on our economy and why it is so important in Michigan. Students had to write a script that would "sell" their location. They had to use their persuasive writing skills to convince the audience that they had the best location in Michigan to visit. **Finally,** we talked a lot about budgeting and planning out the expenses of things to do in the city. Hopefully, they gained some appreciation for how expensive it can be to go on vacation!

Timeline:

1–2 Weeks

Pure Michigan 2.0

The Story:

As mentioned earlier in the book, as we were gearing up to launch this project for the 2019–2020 school year, some big and controversial news hit our state as our Governor vetoed the budget of this successful ad campaign that had run for over a decade. Essentially, with one slash of ink, she would have ended this program if the budget passed. This was the perfect opportunity to jump down a new rabbit hole and take this project in a new direction.

As a class, we watched a bunch of Pure Michigan commercials in class to spark students' interest. I asked them what the purpose of this was, why it mattered, and how tourism impacted Michigan. After a great discussion, without saying anything, I subtly put a newspaper article on the screen showing that the campaign had been canceled. The room erupted in outrage...they were hooked.

Two weeks after completing this project, we had our annual field trip to our state capitol building. We were greeted by our state representative, who taught us about a new bill she was introducing that very day. After talking about the bill and the process for a bill becoming a law, she asked my students if anyone had any questions for her, which opened the door for my students. They began asking her about the Pure Michigan campaign finance debate and why it was being canceled. I could tell she was not expecting these kinds of questions. Still, she was impressed by their passion and knowledge, proving that when we give our young experts the opportunity to engage in authentic learning experiences and dialogue with real experts, the learning feels real and is much more meaningful.

Driving Question:

Our driving questions for this project were pretty simple, "Should the State of Michigan's government fund the Pure Michigan Campaign or not? What implications would it have on our state if it was canceled?"

Learn From Experts:

I reached out to the same expert we had connected with the previous year for our original Pure Michigan Project. Once again, he was able to Skype in and teach us about the implications this budgetary adjustment could have on our state.

Become Experts through Project-Based Learning:

Students had to do an extensive amount of research and form their own opinions on this topic. Since this was such a hot-button issue in Michigan at the time, there were many articles being written in the press, providing lots of reasoning on both sides of the argument. In this circumstance, the research phase of this project did not take very long at all.

Teach Others as Experts:

This is where learning got real. At this same time during writing, we were learning how to write persuasive essays—we couldn't have timed it better. I told students we were going to write persuasive essays to our governor and share our voices with her on this topic. The audience doesn't get more authentic than that!

But to take this one step further, we recorded and published a podcast episode to share our voices with a wider audience on the debate. Our podcast had four sections to it: 1) What is Pure Michigan? 2) How does the tourism industry affect Michigan? 3) Arguments to cancel the Pure Michigan Campaign, and 4) Arguments to fund the Pure Michigan Campaign. I shared this podcast on my social media platforms, and within three days, we had seventy-five listeners. This made students feel heard and that their own recently-gained expertise was valued.

Cross-curricular Connections:

Social Studies and ELA: Study the effect and impact of Michigan's Tourism Industry on our state. Students studied the Pure Michigan Ad Campaign that our state had run for the last ten years. Furthermore, students read many informational articles and had to take notes, consider different viewpoints, make a claim on this topic, and back it up with evidence. Finally, students practiced opinion writing by writing a persuasive essay addressed to our governor.

Timeline:

2 Weeks

Entrepreneur Day

The Story:

Entrepreneur Day was born out of the desire to give students a more authentic way of teaching an economics unit in our social studies curriculum. Instead of reading about how to start a business and what a business plan is, we challenged students to create their own business and learn firsthand. Students started by defining problems in their lives at home or at school and then designed a solution. From there, they created the product, an advertising campaign, and perfected their sales pitch to be ready for the big showcase where the rest of the school would come to "buy" their products.

Driving Question:

How can you create a product or service that will help to solve a problem you've seen or experienced in the world?

Learn From Experts:

One of the challenges of this project is that, as educators, we are not entrepreneurs. We haven't written business plans or started our own businesses. Luckily, through personal and online networks, we were able to connect our students to actual business people with relevant experience. The coolest part of learning from experts, in this case, was when we reached out to the founders of a favorite ed-tech company, Flipgrid, and they Skyped with our students! They were way better at explaining the ins and outs of creating a startup business than we were. Some of our students were able to pitch their product or service ideas to these guests and get feedback from the creators of Flipgrid.

Become Experts through Project-Based Learning:

The project phase of this experience involved brainstorming products, developing prototypes, making constantly improving iterations of the products, and creating Shark Tank-style pitches to present their problem and solution. We've seen so many creative ideas over the years—everything from silly putty for stress relief to lavender-scented aromatherapy jars for decompressing after a test... protective cases for fidget spinners, complete with belt clips and under-desk hook installation services for hanging pencil bags out of the way. The creativity that children will show when you give them a productive challenge is inspiring.

Teach Others as Experts:

The culmination of this project comes from transforming our school cafeteria into a pop-up artisan flea market showcasing the creations of our 4th-grade entrepreneurs. We invite all the other grade-levels in and hand them $20 in "Costello Cardinal Currency," similar to punch cards from a carnival. The entrepreneurs must try their best to convince these K-5 consumers to "buy" their products.

Cross-curricular Connections:

Social Studies, Math, and Writing: Students had to learn the economics of starting a business, including start-up costs and the various types of capital needed, and the fundamental theory of supply and demand. They were also tasked with creating a business plan, a budget, and a cost/profit analysis after the big day, and don't forget the STEAM skills (science, technology, engineering, art, and math) involved with creating the actual product and designing functional improvements over multiple models through the design thinking process. Finally, students employed skills of persuasive writing to write sales pitches and create commercials for our class Seesaw page.

Timeline:

3 Weeks

The Cardboard Challenge

The Story:

As you've probably noticed by this point, one of our most passionate beliefs regarding teaching is that school should be more than just a place for content delivery and instruction. School should be a place that inspires creativity and innovation and prepares young people to be successful in whatever they choose to do after their schooling.

During the first week of school, I (Grayson) brought up the idea of taking on our own version of the Cardboard Challenge, inspired by the video *Caine's Arcade*. If you don't know Caine's amazing story of how he turned his father's Californian car parts shop into a cardboard arcade over summer vacation, watch the video below to learn his story. This short film went viral and has started an entire movement in schools to foster creativity and innovation by taking place in the Cardboard Challenge.

https://youtu.be/Ul9c-4dX4Hk

The premise is simple: have families collect cardboard, tape, and small items to bring into school and create an arcade. Admittedly, we originally thought this would only be fun and games for the kids. We knew that it would get them excited for school but weren't sure what other benefits it would bring. We quickly realized this was an extremely powerful day of learning and the lessons extended so far beyond that which is typically taught in school. Students learned to regroup when their original plan failed, they learned to collaborate with others for parts of their creation, and they learned that failure isn't final. By the end of this day, each student had a successful cardboard arcade game, even if many looked much different from their original plan.

Driving Question:

How can we use our strength of creativity to upcycle everyday objects like cardboard boxes into something of value for the students in our school?

Learn From Experts:

We went right to the source to learn about turning cardboard into arcade games by watching every video that Caine had created, chronicling his inspiration and creative process. Although Caine has since retired from the arcade business, these videos are still available to watch on YouTube. As we watched these videos over the weeks leading up to our day of play, we started to build excitement for this project. As Dave Burgess would say, we were "preheating the grill." We started with a simple planning sheet so students could draw out a blueprint for what they hoped to accomplish and list the materials they would need.

Become Experts through Project-Based Learning:

As teachers, we know that even the best-laid plans can go sideways in a second, but in the Cardboard Challenge, many children learned this valuable lesson firsthand. Once they started building and creating, most students realized that they needed to alter their designs for them to be successful. This was the beauty of it all. Games fell over, didn't work, and needed to change. One thing was for sure though, there was no way any kid was going to give up and not have their game featured in our school arcade later in the day, so they pressed on and found a way to make it work!

We impressed upon our students that to be successful in today's world, you need to stand out, not blend in. Seth Godin coins this concept of being the "Purple Cow," being remarkable in whatever you do. In the Cardboard Challenge, kids wanted their games to stand out; they wanted to be different. This is a lesson that would never have been learned if our school's classrooms had been filled with fill-in-the-blank worksheets. Our students became problem-solvers like the astronauts of Apollo 13...creating success on a wing and a prayer (and lots and lots of duct tape)!

Teach Others as Experts:

As we said, most of the designs were unsuccessful after the first attempts, or students found some design flaw that required a change. This taught them that just because it didn't work the first time, it didn't mean the game was doomed. The students were ready to teach others about their own experience when we finally invited the whole school down to our gymnasium to let them play the games. The teaching as experts happened every time a student came to play. Students would have to explain the rules of the game, how they created it, and the setbacks they faced. Throughout the afternoon, they had dozens of interactions with other kids from around the school and, in the process, refined their "boardwalk barker" speech.

There is a lot of teaching happening in schools today about the value of failing and having a growth mindset. While we think the message of "we should celebrate failures" can be taken a little out of context, what we really need to do is help students recognize authentically that just because you made a mistake doesn't mean they are a personal failure! The Cardboard Challenge helped them see this. They were in a safe space to make mistakes and improve upon them.

Finally, after participating in the Cardboard Challenge for multiple years in a row, we wanted to give our veteran cardboard creators the chance to experience the process from a different angle—fifth-graders who had built games as fourth-graders were given a chance to help mentor a second-grade class who was doing their own cardboard engineering. Pairing up older students with younger ones was just one more avenue for students to become experts and impart wisdom and advice (and the hand strength it takes to cut through thick cardboard).

Cross-curricular Connections:

STEAM: Usually, if someone says they're doing something STEAM-related, they pick and choose which letters to focus on for a given project. The cardboard challenge, however, was a project that hit on every letter in the STEAM acronym! The science of upcycling instead of throwing cardboard away, the technology to plan out their design and materials to be used, the engineering to build and rebuild their concept, the art to make their game and display pleasing to the eye and attractive to their customers, and the math involved in keeping score on various games...plus the counting up of all the quarters collected to be donated to Caine's educational foundation, imagination.org.

Timeline:

1–2 Weeks

Costello Developer Academy and Expo

The Story:

In the fall of 2018, Zach and I attended an educational conference in Chicago at Apple's executive headquarters, a beautiful and sterile office space with floor-to-ceiling windows overlooking the Chicago River.

The purpose of the conference was to learn about Apple's approach to teaching computer science and app coding to kindergarten through 12th-grade students. Throughout the process, we worked closely with our district superintendent and building principal to hone our department of teaching and learning's vision for using these 21st-century skills to provide opportunities for all students to connect to their learning in a meaningful and passionate way.

To do this, we sought to leverage coding and computational thinking skills to empower our students to *own* and *deepen* their learning, giving them yet another avenue to become lifelong learners, critical thinkers, and productive contributors to our global society.

In the winter of that school year, the two of us turned our classrooms into deep-learning laboratories around coding and app design, creating what we dubbed the "Costello Developer Academy." This program was established to allow students to experience the design-thinking process and get to know some basic coding principles.

Driving Question:

This driving question was posted in our classrooms and referred back to often throughout the Academy: "How can thinking like an app developer lead to solving problems and making a positive impact on the world?" By framing the question like this and doing so early on in the process, it gave context to all of the coding activities our students would undertake. We challenged them to be content creators—not just consumers—who could add something of value to the world around them through their unique app ideas.

Learn From Experts:

One of the challenges of this project was that we, as teachers, did not have a coding background. One of the common myths in education is that teachers must be an expert on every subject. Instead of only taking the kids as far as we could with our limited know-how, we decided to reach out to create local partnerships in the community so they (our community partners) could be the experts our students relied on to help them through their acquisition of coding knowledge and through the app development process. We took our students to a local mall to the Apple and Microsoft stores. Working with a team of these experts in the Microsoft store, students learned how to code their own basic video games. In the Apple store, students learned how to use the program Keynote to develop a working app prototype. This was an incredible and invaluable learning opportunity—over the next few weeks taking on a life of its own in our classrooms.

In the Apple workshop, students learned from the resident "geniuses" the 4 stages of the App Design Cycle, and below we will break down each stage of the process.

1. Brainstorm
2. Plan
3. Prototype
4. Evaluate

In the Brainstorming phase, students were encouraged to develop their sense of empathy and step inside the shoes of a person or group of people in the world who may be experiencing a problem. By answering three simple questions, "Who is your app for?", "What will your app help people do?" and "How will your app help them?", our learners were able to develop their app definition statement. Having a clear goal for supporting a discrete group of people helped to narrow the focus of their design efforts.

In the evaluation phase, students passed their prototype creation to other peers and let them work their way through the app. Many times, students found broken links or "bugs" to report back. Students provided authentic feedback to their peers to improve their prototypes.

As another aspect of the evaluation phase, we reached out to the high school AP Computer Science teacher, Mr. Josh Pudaloff (@jpudaloff), who had been working with his own high schoolers all year to create and code actual apps. He brought his class to walk around our rooms and provide feedback to our young developers on what they created. This was another way to make it real for our students and provide more opportunities for connection and collaboration with real-life experts.

Become Experts through Project-Based Learning:

Students used Keynote on the iPad to create a prototype that looked and functioned like an actual app. By creating on-screen buttons and using the built-in hyperlinking features of Keynote, students could design their prototype so that different buttons would lead to different places like pictures, videos, websites, or additional menus and text. Creating linear slideshows is one thing, a relatively low-level task on the SAMR spectrum, but asking students to plan the flow of their app with multiple pathways to follow created a significant opportunity for students to think multi-dimensionally, with links acting like a Choose Your Own Adventure Book. Part of the students' enthusiasm for this project was derived from the increased level of complexity that their app prototypes could demonstrate. We created a group of non-linear thinkers, helping them to develop a capacity for problem-solving that extended in multiple directions. Rather than thinking step-by-step and moving in one direction, our students were given the opportunity to see that there are multiple starting points from which one can apply the solution to a problem. The students loved this, and it definitely made their creations feel real.

One of our favorite ways to judge the quality of our assigned projects is based on students' willingness to work on it outside of school, even when it's not required. For these two weeks, students were coming in each morning excited to show the new feature they had added at home. It soon became a competition to see how many separate slides and links and pseudo-animations they had come up with. Students would design and redesign their app logos using Canva until they were perfect and presentable. When students care about what they're creating, they become unstoppable. It's best to get out of their way, simply offering guidance and support as needed.

After many cycles of evaluation and iteration, students created a "final prototype" (probably an oxymoron) that they felt comfortable show-casing to the world.

Teach Others as Experts:

Finally, the big day had arrived! Part of our classroom philosophy that certainly carried over to our Developers Academy is that we firmly believe in giving our students as many opportunities as possible to present their learning to authentic audiences. As you know by now, we believe creating an event for students and inviting in outside people boosts the engagement and excitement, and therefore the learning for students. As such, we invited our Superintendent, Board of Education members, district technology leaders, as well as our district's media department to take pictures and document the big day.

We started out with a bang by inviting a select number of students from our fourth- and fifth-grade classes to give an opening keynote address. We coached them to prepare for this moment by showing them TED talks and examples of students giving keynote speeches, including our favorite of all time, Dalton Sherman's "Do You Believe in Me?" keynote speech.

We asked them to share the process we had gone through to get to that point so that our outside guests would have some background knowledge of all the learning that took place until that point. I wish we had recorded it because the students did an amazing job. The rest of the students sat patiently, listening to their peers recount their experience while the guests got caught up on the undertaking. They shared the process, owned the learning, and started the expo in a Steve Jobs-fashion.

Next, developers headed off to their stations, where they had their iPads displayed for visitors to try out their apps while they explained the thoughts behind their creation. They also had created a poster version of an App Store "review," in which they had classmates review their app, give a description of the purpose, and recommend an age for the user, based on the social media "features," such as texting and access to the web that they included.

Cross-curricular Connections:

ELA and STEAM: One of the biggest values and selling points of this academy format for us as regular classroom teachers was the planning phase. It was in this part of our project that we were able to get students to really connect the computer science side of things to what they were already learning curriculum-wise. In their planning, we asked students to think about what information or content their app would need to be pre-loaded with. Were they designing an app to end world hunger? Then they would need to have intimate knowledge about this global issue in order to be able to solve it. Developing an app to help predict severe weather and other natural disasters? Then the students' knowledge of meteorology was an essential part of the app! It is through this type of Project-Based Learning that students begin to realize what they don't know already and what they need to find out.

Timeline:

Over four months, the students extensively used two apps, Tynker and CodeSpark Academy, to learn the basic coding concepts. It was only in the final two weeks that they took what they knew and created their own functioning app prototype, received feedback from peers and high school students, and made changes before finally presenting their work at the expo. Below is a video created by our school district during the showcase of this expo and something we are both very proud of.

https://youtu.be/Omr4y0_3ako

The Westward Expansion Film Festival

The Story:

Part of our fifth-grade English Language Arts curriculum involves students researching and writing about the period of American History when the general electorate was moving westward, filled with dreams of striking it rich during the California Goldrush or staking out a fertile homestead at the end of the Oregon Trail. While I (Grayson) never had any trouble getting excited about heading west on an 8-bit wagon train, thanks to the version of the selfsame video game loaded on my elementary school's Macintosh Classics in 1992, my students' enthusiasm was for a more modern computer game: Minecraft. Armed with a little knowledge about this super-popular video game and its ability to be easily-integrated into academics, I made an attempt to merge the two to create an engaging and memorable experience.

Minecraft: Education Edition is an open-world game that promotes creativity, collaboration, and problem-solving where the only limit is your imagination. The number one concern that we hear from teachers through Twitter, Facebook, conferences, and face-to-face conversations is, "That's great for you, but it won't work in my classroom." Whether this trepidation comes from a lack of content knowledge, classroom management skills, significantly needier populations of students, or simply feeling like there's too much to get done to allow time for projects and other big commitments, our advice is this: Think big, start small. While this may seem like nothing but a trite expression, it's really true and a savvy bit of wisdom.

Learn From Experts:

Before we could dive into the fun of building and surviving in the world of Minecraft, we had to immerse ourselves in the history of our country. We read primary documents in the form of diaries of pioneers headed west. We read books written from the perspective of prospectors headed out to live on the prairies. But the most impactful learning experience, the ones that our students gained the most insight from, was discussing life on a wagon train from an "actual" wagon master from the Oregon Trail Museum in Idaho. This expert worked day-in and day-out explaining to paying tourists how and why the settlers were moving west, but we were able to Skype with him from in front of his "prairie schooner" on a slow day at the museum.

After talking to one expert on life and death on the wagon trail, we also wanted to learn more about the land they were moving to, and how the environment gave them challenges and the resources they needed to make a new start. We Skyped with the staff at the highly engaging Wyoming Museum of Natural History. We learned about the animals they found out west, and even about the forts they built along the way.

To get experience navigating around the world of Minecraft, we even explored an interactive learning simulation built right into the game. Using the interactive Oregon Trail world, students were able to walk through and interact with NPCs, or non-player characters, click on hyperlinks that took them outside the game for further reading, and traveled along in the shoes of their virtual avatars in our virtual field trip. We started in Independence, Missouri, and ended in Oregon City, Oregon, where they built a cabin to call their very own.

Become Experts through Project-Based Learning:

Once we had learned from experts (both human and NPC alike), we were ready to use Minecraft to "craft" scenes that we had researched and to show what we had learned. Students created replica forts like Fort Laramie and navigational landmarks like Chimney Rock and Independence Rock. Other scenes they made included a wagon train robbery by outlaws, while another group created an interactive diorama that other students could "visit" to learn the difference between fording and floating dangerous river crossings that wagoners would have encountered. Then they screen-captured these vignettes and edited them together into a 30-minute film on the various aspects of moving out west.

We had done it! We had used technology to emulate what it would have been like to come to a new land with nothing but the clothes on our backs and a virtual wilderness before us. We were allowed to step inside the people we were learning about and empathize with what life must have been like for them at the time.

Teach Others as Experts:

We sent our video to school groups we had previously connected with in Canada and New York to teach other students what we had learned. We uploaded this video to YouTube so that future generations of researchers (and Minecrafters) could learn from students' experience, like a graduate student who sees their thesis published and available to check out from the university's library…but more fun! Needless to say, the kids have been hooked ever since the day we opened the Pandora's box that is Minecraft.

At a recent visit made by teachers and administrators from our neighboring school districts, several students in my class wanted to present what we had done and what we learned through our use of Minecraft. They put together an abbreviated video walk-through of our world, a Keynote presentation showing the stages of development and the problems that arose, and a poster with some key social studies ideas that developed naturally through our use of the simulation.

Timeline:

4 Weeks

https://youtu.be/8XcxXSbxdj4

Welcome to the Neighborhood

The Story:

This example comes from a second-grade classroom in our school. The teacher, Mrs. Lindsey Maliepaard, was in the midst of a social studies unit in which students were being tasked to learn about the community in which they live: Troy, Michigan. In order to make this topic more relevant and meaningful, she wanted to set the learning into the context of helping a family that was considering moving to one of two communities in the United States from South Korea. The family (which may or may not have been fictitious) needed to consider the types of things that make a community a community—public safety, quality education, growing job market, affordable housing—and had to choose between Troy, Michigan, and Orangeburg, South Carolina (a city to which a former classmate had just recently moved).

Driving Question:

How can we use our learning in social studies to make a difficult decision easier for a family that's considering moving into our community?

Learn From Experts:

Lindsey cast a wide net in looking for experts that could help her make the topic of a community come to life for her second graders. The first person they talked to was a local realtor to share housing options in Troy and help compare them to housing options in South Carolina. They also pulled in our school superintendent, Dr. Richard Machesky, to help them learn about what makes the Troy School District (TSD) stand out from other local school districts, how the schools support families learning English as a second language, and other statistics that make TSD well-known and world-class. Students also drafted questions to ask a member of our Troy Police Department to learn more about the safety of our community and why anyone moving from out of the country should pick Troy as their new place to call home. Finally, a fourth expert was involved, a representative from the Troy Community Center, to learn more about all of the options available to Troy residents such as games, sports, language learning, family events and more.

Become Experts through Project-Based Learning:

Students used all the data collected to make short commercial-like videos full of information about Troy that would help the family from Korea to learn about our community and make an informed decision about their big move to the United States.

Teach Others as Experts:

For this project, the audience was defined as a family being moved from South Korea to the United States because of the father's job with an automobile company.

Cross-curricular Connections:

Writing, Reading, and Social Studies: In order to create the most "bang-for-your-buck," it always makes sense to try and tie it into more than one area of content learning...not only to justify the time and effort it takes to make projects successful, but also simultaneously make multiple content areas relevant. For this activity, while Social Studies was the main focus—learning about our local community through geography, civics, and inquiry—she also chose to incorporate aspects of her then-current writing unit, persuasive writing (forming an opinion and supporting it with specific evidence). Furthermore, as with all forms of inquiry-based learning, reading of informational texts was also essential.

Timeline:

6 Weeks

Project-Based Learning: Real Talk

While projects like these can be quite a large undertaking, we always feel they are completely worth it in the end because they are memorable learning experiences that will stick with kids long past the time they leave our classrooms. Because of that, they are projects we would gladly commit to doing again year after year. While not every student will grow up to be a computer programmer, entrepreneur, podcast host, or real estate agent, the principles that were elevated, such as gaining content knowledge, enhancing communication skills, and discovering a sense of agency for solving real-world problems, will help our students to become empowered and adaptive workers in whatever field they find themselves in.

We want them to be able to shape the world around them—not just be shaped by it. Asking yourself the simple questions of "Who can we learn from and who can we teach?" will set your class up for memorable learning opportunities. We want to help you to feel confident planning your lessons...units...years through the lens of *The Expert Effect*. For your convenience, we've included a template below to help you plan out your own learning experiences. You can access a blank copy from the QR Code to have a clean copy to use over and over and over!

Expert Effect Planning Document

Expert Effect Planning Document	
Driving Question for the Project:	
Phase 1: **Learn From** **Experts**	1. To what outside experts can you connect your students to deepen their learning? 2. Who could you ask to speak to your class virtually or in person? 3. Check out the Microsoft in Education website. What virtual field trips could you set up to enhance an already existing lesson or unit you teach? 4. What places might you take a virtual field trip to help students understand more? Look it up or reach out, it could be easier to arrange than you think! 5. What places or experiences are in your curriculum that you could have students "travel" to using virtual reality? 6. What field trips close to school could you take to enhance learning for your students?
Phase 2: **Students Become** **the Expert**	1. What area of your existing curriculum do you think you can incorporate Project Based Learning? 2. What product can students create to show their learning? (blog, website, live skit, Keynote/Powerpoint presentation, iMovie, board game, eBook, write a song, etc) 3. How can you give students/groups different options to showcase their learning?
Phase 3: **Teach as an** **Expert**	1. What authentic audience can you find for your students to present their learning to? 2. Who in your immediate school setting can you recruit as an audience for your students? Who could you recruit from your central office? Local government? 3. Who can you recruit virtually who would be interested in hearing your students' ideas? Dream big! (A marine biologist for a science project, a historian for a social studies project, don't be afraid to ask!)
Cross-Curricular **Connections**	What content is being taught during this entire process? How can you tie in multiple subject areas?

Expert Effect Planning Document

Driving Question for the Project:	
Phase 1: Learn From Experts	
Phase 2: Students Become the Expert	
Phase 3: Teach as an Expert	
Cross-Curricular Connections	

CONCLUSION

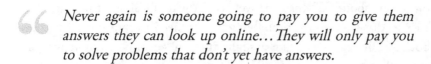 *Never again is someone going to pay you to give them answers they can look up online...They will only pay you to solve problems that don't yet have answers.*

–SETH GODIN

Teaching is one of the most difficult and dynamic careers that exist. Overcrowding of our classrooms, a persistent lack of support staff to meet the needs of all learners, overworked and underpaid teachers, and PANDEMICS, on top of underfunded schools, all lead to a perfect storm that drives thousands of professionals out of the system every year. Our goal of educating children has been likened to trying to nail Jell-O to a wall... except the wall is crumbling, and your school doesn't supply you with the hammers.

We hope that by introducing you to a new way to approach the process of teaching and learning by getting your students to learn from experts outside of the classroom, become experts through Project-Based Learning, and teach others as experts to an authentic audience, we are setting you up with a winning formula to achieve the desired results—not just the memorization of your curriculum, but the ignition of a passion for learning where students see themselves as individuals who deserve to learn from the best, become the best, and improve the world through their learning. We know firsthand that changing our way of thinking about teaching in this way has reignited our passion in the classroom.

When we talk to other teachers about what we're having our students do during class time, the biggest question we get is, "That's great for you, but how do I fit that into our schedule? We don't have time for that kind of thing." Back in the old days, teachers would teach a unit and then, after all of the learning was done, have students complete a fun "dessert" project...or even worse...as extra credit! This is where the secret of Project-Based Learning becomes so important! Projects can't be an afterthought and happen as extra work after the "learning" (memorization, really) has taken place. For us, projects are the "main course" and the WHY for the learning. In our classrooms, we don't say, "You've learned all about *X*, so now you're going to do a project to show what you know about *X*." Instead, we say, "You're all about to create *Y* in order to do *Z*, so you're probably going to need to find out all you can about *X*!" It may seem like a slight shift in semantics, but it makes a world of difference in terms of student motivation and execution. We tell everyone who will listen that this shift in how you frame the learning leads to the four Rs: increased "Rigor" of learning, better "Relationships" among your students and the wider community, instant "Relevance" of what you're trying to teach them, and simply awesome "Results" in what the children will produce. When you set high expectations for learning while supporting students with a rigorous and innovative instructional framework, we have found, again and again, that when you give students the opportunity to amaze you, they usually do.

WHEN YOU GIVE STUDENTS THE OPPORTUNITY TO AMAZE YOU, THEY USUALLY DO.
#ExpertEffectEDU

From beginning to end, we help kids learn curricular concepts, get enthusiastic about their learning, help them create prototypes through the design thinking process, and then discover that they can use all that to make a difference in the world. It doesn't get much better than that!

We've given you our take on this process and shared examples of how we've implemented this pedagogy in our own school setting, but now it's time to give you a taste of what the students themselves think of learning in this way because they are the ones we are asking to live through it. No matter the obstacles, they're never going to take away the power of kids' imagination. And as we stated in the dedication of this book, it is these stories of our own students and their unstoppable creativity that we want to share with the world.

> *I know firsthand the effort that is necessary to master new things. I've learned that if I'm dedicated, if I'm motivated, if I'm passionate about learning, then I can do it.*
>
> —ERIC, CLASS OF 2026

> *I have learned that when I'm working to make something better than anything I've ever made, I (or we) have to be committed to seeing our vision come to life. We have the chance to change the world.*
>
> —EKAANSH, CLASS OF 2026

> *Anybody can change the world through the creation of something, like an app, for instance. If they're an adult or kids like us, they can study, they can learn, and they can use what they know to make a difference in the world.*
>
> —OLIVIA, CLASS OF 2026

Sometimes it's hard to make a difference in the world because there's a whole big world, and you can't travel to all the countries, but you CAN use your voice, and your voice can be heard all around the world through a podcast or a blog post.

–BELLA, CLASS OF 2027

We would be remiss if we left you at the end of this book thinking that turning your classroom into a well-oiled *Expert Effect* machine would go smoothly—business as usual without any unforeseen consequences. We hate to break it to you, but there are some side effects of moving towards this mentality. Like any responsible entity, it's our job to inform you of all that can happen when you embrace this model of teaching. But we don't call them side effects; we call them *Expert Effects!*

Expert Effect #1: Selective Perfectionism

When students have a reason for stepping it up and creating something that has the potential to change the world—or at least change the lives of someone they care about—they are much more willing to do what it takes to create a quality product to showcase their learning. When they know that what they create, whether it be a video, slideshow, a story, a podcast, or a new app prototype, is going to be viewed, read, listened to, or used by someone out in the world, they want to make it the best it can be. Students who may not always be so fastidious become "selective perfectionists" when the stage is set just right.

Expert Effect #2: A Deep Love for Learning

Think of your curriculum as a mountain bike path through the woods. As you and all the other teachers in your building set off down this trail, you will undoubtedly be at different levels of experience and comfort. Some of you will stick to the well-worn path, starting at the start and ending at the finish, having covered the distance prescribed by the scope and sequence of your curriculum. Some of the "bikers" will veer off the course here and there, testing out the shocks as they roll over ruts and roots. Will they still reach the end? Undoubtedly they will, while getting some "mud on the tires" along the way. Then there are those who will use the curriculum as an opportunity to go deeper into the woods. Following the paths less traveled, they will find the twists and turns along the way invigorating—the switchbacks and the tabletops, narrow bridges, and even the uphill climbs as a challenge worth taking on.

When you use your curriculum not as a script or recipe, but rather as a diving board, you demonstrate a deep love of learning that students can't help but feel and eventually emulate. After going through this process of inquiry-based learning with our students, we can tell you that it becomes the habitual culture of the classroom to expect that learning can go deeper than skimming the surface. Students begin to think of every lesson in terms of, "How can I use my learning to improve the world around me? Who can I learn from if I want to know more?" A chapter from a social studies book might become a podcast episode in the making. A science lesson might become a research project to find answers to the questions newly generated. An exploration of bar graphs in math could transform the classroom into a capitalistic microeconomy.

Expert Effect #3: High Engagement

As anyone who has spent time around young people or has been a young person themselves will know, children's levels of engagement thrive on novelty. When there is anything even slightly new or unusual, levels of engagement will go through the roof. Part of the benefit of giving students the chance to learn from experts inside and outside of the class-room is the simple fact that they are learning from a new person. If you have ever come to school the day after getting a new haircut or having shaved off a beard or wearing a new pair of shoes, you know what we're talking about. Kids look at you like you're an alien with three heads. Have you ever run into a student at the grocery store? It's like their universe has been turned upside down. Left is right, right is wrong, and all because of the novelty effect.

Harnessing the inherent power of originality and newness can create memorable learning experiences. Looking at a picture of a reptile in a textbook or on an iPad can be fun, but wrapping a 100-pound snake around students' shoulders is even more so (or at least more terrifying). Reading about the Revolutionary War can be interesting, but Skyping with an educator at the Museum of the American Revolution would bring that history to life in a way that merely reading about it never could.

Expert Effect #4: Empowered Learners

If there is one end-goal that education should strive for, it would be to create students who are empowered learners. We want to guide students to the knowledge, confidence, means, and ability to do things and make decisions for themselves. When we attempt to define what that actually looks like in schools, the *Expert Effect* comes to mind: empowering our students to learn from, become, and teach others as experts. While we can't tell you exactly who they should learn from or who they should teach, we do believe that whoever you decide on, it will help to generate new knowledge, give them the confidence to interact with others, and grant them the chance to be creators, not just consumers, who are free to pursue their own lines of inquiry to slake their curiosities. In our humble opinion, it's better to be the one who poses new questions than the one who memorizes old answers. Learning to ask important questions, after all, is the best evidence of understanding there is.

Expert Effect #5: Kids Who Are Excited to Come to School

It's Entrepreneur Day! It's Lumberjack Day! It's time for the Cardboard Challenge! The Developer Academy Expo is this afternoon! In the same way that the turning of the calendar from holiday to holiday can mark the passage of time, celebrations of learning make the school year fly by. Building in regular opportunities for students to learn from experts and occasions during which students can showcase their learning can keep school exciting and meaningful for even the most reluctant learner. It also gives students more opportunities to become better presenters, effecting meaningful learning experiences for their audiences.

Expert Effect #6: A Better Work Environment for You!

Let's face it. Motivated students are happy, engaged students. Why would it be any different for you? When you are able to connect your students to an authentic, real-world situation that demands critical thinking, creativity, and collaboration, so many classroom issues simply melt away. You reach a special level of positive energy when there's a synergy between the teacher and students. This interaction and cooperation produce a combined effect greater than the sum of their separate interests.

Regardless of what content area or age you teach, you have the fulfilling responsibility of opening pathways for young people to make a positive impact on the world. Too often, teachers fail to connect content to the real world and the issues that exist there. We have the chance to positively impact the future of our world eight hours a day, five days a week. We have the constant opportunity to bring new ideas and new ways of thinking into a society that would otherwise stagnate at the status quo. In many ways, teaching is the only hope that humanity has for creating a sustainable, equitable future. At the end of the day, we all want to make a difference in the lives of children.

If you can tie what you're doing back to one or more of these three pillars, you're doing something right. Our hope is that by giving your students the chance to learn from experts near and far, become experts through their own cycles of inquiry, and teach others as experts, they will be fulfilling that mission statement—improving their own lives, the lives of others, and the world around them. If they do, you'll be fulfilling the goal of our profession, keeping the lamplight of hope lit in the ever-encroaching darkness. You and your students are proof that humanity can still redeem itself. We are grateful for you, and the world will be too!

ABOUT THE AUTHORS

Zach Rondot, M.A.

Zach Rondot is a passionate fourth-grade teacher in Troy, Michigan. His mission is to teach students the mindsets, skills, and attributes that will help them live a happy, successful, and fulfilling life long after they leave his classroom. Zach is known for his positivity and being a true agent for change. Zach was named 2019 Troy School District Elementary Teacher of the Year as well as the 2019 Oakland County Elementary Teacher of the Year.

Zach has a Master's Degree in Educational Technology from Central Michigan University and is also an adjunct faculty instructor in the Master's program of Learning, Design, and Technology at CMU. He utilizes technology to create learning opportunities that otherwise would not be possible. Zach and his students created The *4th-Grade Innovators Podcast* with the aim to inspire, motivate, and make a positive impact on kids and adults around the world. The podcast has been listened to in Australia, Africa, Europe, Asia, and all over North America. Check it out at Anchor.fm/4thgradeinnovators

Zach is a dynamic presenter who has been featured at various educational conferences, universities, and Edcamps over the last five years. He loves connecting with teachers around the world to grow his Professional Learning Network. Connect with Zach at his blog, ZachRondot.com, on Clubhouse: @MrRondot, on Twitter: @MrRondot, or on Instagram: @ZachRondot.

Grayson McKinney,
Ed.S.

Grayson McKinney is an elementary educator from East Grand Rapids, Michigan. His mission as a teacher is to empower students to connect their learning to the world in order to improve their own lives, improve the lives of others, and improve the environment around them. Grayson is known for his innovative approaches to teaching and learning and is a true agent for change. Grayson was named 2012 Elementary Teacher of the Year in the South Lake School District.

Grayson has shared his expertise and knowledge at various universities, conferences, and Edcamps around the Midwest, speaking on topics including increasing student voice, providing learners with authentic audiences, mindfulness in the classroom, technology integration, gamification of curriculum, harnessing the power of social media to be a digital leader, creating a digital culture of thinking and innovation, and innovating student assessment through Project-Based Learning and portfolio building.

Grayson attended Western Michigan University as an undergraduate and went on to earn his Master's and Education Specialist Degrees in School Leadership from Oakland University. He is both an Apple Teacher as well as a Microsoft Innovative Educator and an ambassador for several other educational technology companies. Grayson and his students created The *5th-Grade Futurists Podcast* with the aim to spread awareness of the United Nations' 17 Global Goals for a Sustainable Future around the world. Check out his students' voices here: anchor.fm/thefuturist5.

Grayson is an enthusiastic presenter who loves connecting with educators to grow his professional learning family. You can connect with Grayson at his blog, innovation4education.wordpress.com, on Clubhouse: @GMcKinney2, on Twitter: @GMcKinney2, or on Instagram: @ExpertEffectEDU.

REFERENCES

Introduction

Couros, G. (2015). The innovator's mindset: Empower learning, unleash talent, and lead a culture of creativity. San Diego, CA: Dave Burgess Consulting, Inc.

Muir, T. (2014, November.) Trevor Muir: School should take place in the real world. TedxSanAntonio Retrieved from https://www.youtube.com/watch?v=9ei_HSlUxUQ

Chapter One

Fall enrollments decline for 8th consecutive year. (2019, December). Retrieved from www.studentclearinghouse.org/nscblog/fall-enrollments-decline-for-8th-consecutive-year/

Godin, S. (2010). Linchpin: Are you indispensable? *New York, NY: Penguin Publishing Group.*

Linder, C. (2019, November 4). *This 14-year-old science fair winner just solved blind spots. Retrieved from https://www.popularmechanics.com/cars/car-technology/a29668880/eliminate-blind-spot/*

Manyika, J., Chui, M., Bughin, J., Dobbs, R., Bisson, P., & Marrs, A. (May 2013). Disruptive technologies: Advances that will transform life, business, and the global economy. Retrieved from https://www.mckinsey.com/business-functions/mckinsey-digital/our-insights/disruptive-technologies#

Miller, C. (2018, September 10). Does teacher diversity matter in student learning? Retrieved from https://www.nytimes.com/2018/09/10/upshot/teacher-diversity-effect-students-learning.html

National Center for Education Statistics. (2015). Retrieved December 15, 2019, from https://www.cde.state.co.us/cdereval/nces

Robinson, K. (2006, February). Sir Ken Robinson: Do schools kill creativity? [Video file]. Retrieved from: https://www.ted.com/talks/sir_ken_robinson_do_schools_kill_creativity.

Chapter Two

Busteed, B. (2013, January 7). *The school cliff: Student engagement drops with each school year. Retrieved July 13, 2020, from https://news.gallup.com/ opinion/gallup/170525/school-cliff-student-engagement-drops-school-year.aspx*

Gray, P. (2008, August 20). *A brief history of education. Retrieved September 15, 2019, from https://www. psychologytoday.com/us/blog/freedom-learn/ 200808/brief-history-education*

Chapter Four

Geurin, D. (2017). *Future driven: Will your students thrive in an unpredictable world? Bolivar, MO: David Geurin.*

Chapter Five

Fullan, M., & Quinn, J. (2016). Coherence: The right drivers in action for schools, districts, and systems. *Thousand Oaks, CA: Corwin.*

Hattie, J. (2015). What works best in education: The politics of collaborative expertise, *London, England: Pearson.*

Robinson, K., & Aronica, L. (2015). Creative schools: The grassroots revolution that's transforming education. *[Audible audiobook]. Retrieved from http://www.audible.com*

Skype in the Classroom Website: https://education. microsoft.com/skype-in-the-classroom/overview

Chapter Six

Behrendt, M. & Franklin, T.. (2014). A review of research on school field trips and their value in education. International Journal of Environmental and Science Education, 9, *235–245.*

Chapter Seven

Online field trips boost reading scores. (2015, September 2). Retrieved September 28, 2019, from https:// www.eschoolnews.com/2005/05/19/online-field-trips-boost-reading-scores/

Ritchhart, R., & Church, M. (2020). The power of making thinking visible: Practices to engage and empower all learners. *San Francisco, CA: Jossey-Bass.*

Reinicke, C. (2018, July 19). US income inequality continues to grow. Retrieved July 15, 2020, from https://www.cnbc.com/2018/07/19/income-inequality-continues-to-grow-in-the-united-states.html

Chapter Eight

Behrendt, M., & Franklin T. (2014). A review of research on school field trips and their value in education. International Journal of Environmental and Science Education, 9*(3), 235–245. https://files. eric.ed.gov/fulltext/EJ1031445.pdf*

Clewell, S. (2005). *Study: Online field trips boost reading scores.* eSchool News, 8(7), 10. https://www.eschoolnews.com/2005/05/19/online-field-trips-boost-reading-scores/

McRainey, D & Russick, John. (2010). *Connecting kids to history with museum exhibitions. Walnut Creek, CA: Left Coast Press.*

Oyler, M. (2014). *Does the use of virtual field trips increase vocabulary and comprehension for students with disabilities? Retrieved from https://www.nwmissouri.edu/library/researchpapers/2014/Oyler,%20Mary.pdf*

Viswanath, K., & Finnegan Jr., J. R. (1996). *The knowledge gap hypothesis: Twenty-five years later. In B. R. Burleson (Ed.),* Communication yearbook 19 (pp. 187–227). *Thousand Oaks, CA: Sage.*

Chapter Ten

Skype in the Classroom Website: https://education.skype.com/.

Chapter Eleven

Hallermann, S., Larmer, J., & Mergendoller, J. R. (2016). Pbl in the elementary grades: Step-by-step guidance, tools, and tips for standards-focused K–5 projects. *Novato, CA: Buck Institute for Education.*

Lamar, J, Boss, S. (n.d.). *Gold Standard PBL: Essential project design elements. Retrieved from https://www. pblworks.org/what-is-pbl/gold-standard-project-design*

Muir, T. (2018, October 24). *The difference between project-based learning and doing projects. Retrieved from https://trevormuir.com/2018/10/24/dessert-projects/*

Chapter Twelve

Common Core State Standards. (2009). Knowledge of language *(CCSS.ELA-LITERACY.L.5.3). Retrieved from http://www.corestandards.org/ELA-Literacy/L/5/*

Flanagan, N. (2012, January 17). *The problem with lesson plans. Retrieved from http://blogs.edweek.org/ teachers/teacher_in_a_strange_land/2012/01/ the_problem_with_lesson_plans.html? plckFindCommentKey=CommentKey:3f722ad0-fb61-4c9d-b8ab-11483b7f70be*

Marzano, R. J., Pickering, D., & Heflebower, T. (2013). The highly engaged classroom. *United States: No Publisher.*

Spencer, J. (2018, November 30). *Making time for project-based learning. Retrieved from https:// spencerauthor.com/pbl-time/*

Werkhoven, R. *Creativity Requires Time. https://www. youtube.com/watch?v=WDngw5R32WE*

Chapter Thirteen

Puentedura, R. (2009, February 4). As we may teach: Educational technology, from theory into practice. Retrieved from http://hippasus.com/blog/archives/25

Chapter Fourteen

Glass, G. V. (n.d.). School reform proposals: Grouping students for instruction. Retrieved August 20, 2020, from https://nepc.colorado.edu/sites/default/files/Chapter05-Glass-Final.pdf

Weatherby, J. [@JWeatherby]. (2019, May 8). Joanne Weatherby on Twitter. Retrieved from https://twitter.com/JWeatherby/status/1126274403958870016

Chapter Fifteen

Lamar, J., & Boss, S. (n.d.). Gold Standard PBL: Essential project design elements. Retrieved from https://www.pblworks.org/what-is-pbl/gold-standard-project-design

Chapter Sixteen

Burgess, D. (2012). Teach like a pirate: Increase student engagement, boost your creativity, and transform your life as an educator. San Diego, CA: Dave Burgess Consulting, Inc.

EduMatch Publishing

CPSIA information can be obtained
at www.ICGtesting.com
Printed in the USA
BVHW042338070521
606760BV00007B/1750